Sacred Soil

A GARDENER'S BOOK
OF REFLECTION

Sacred Soil

A GARDENER'S BOOK
OF REFLECTION

Melina Rudman

ANAMCHARA
BOOKS

ANAMCHARA BOOKS
Vestal, New York 13850
www.AnamcharaBooks.com

Paperback ISBN: 978-1-62524-516-8
Ebook ISBN: 978-1-62524-517-5

Cover design by Ellyn Sanna.
Interior layout by Micaela Grace.
Illustrations by Micaela Grace.

CONTENTS

Artist's Statement

I write to discover what I know.

(FLANNERY O'CONNOR)

My writing is the voice of spirit speaking in, and to, my life. I write to explore and understand things I know at levels beyond, or perhaps before, cognition. Writing is the vehicle I use to bring what I know intuitively out into the world of words and matter.

My writing process is long and, almost wholly, internal. I see, I think, I wonder and ponder. Ideas and revelations percolate in me as if I were an old-time coffee pot set upon a hot stove. Often weeks or months will

Everything that slows us down and forces patience, everything that sets us back into the slow circles of nature, is a help. Gardening is an instrument of grace.

(MAY SARTON)

find me in this phase until, at last, the "coffee" is made, and the words pour out.

Gardening is also a spiritual practice for me. It is prayer. It grounds me in the seasons and cycles of Nature. It takes me out of the world of ideas and ether, and plants me firmly in the dirt, in the messy circle of birth, life, and death. On my knees in the soil, pulling weeds or crooning to an ailing tomato or cucumber, I am smack dab in the middle of life's gore and glory.

Gardening focuses my attention on what is right before me. It has taught me about my own endurance; it has taught me to let go.

I garden out of a desire for beauty, for resilience, and as a balm for all the wounds inflicted upon me and on Nature, by our busy, capitalist world. I write for some of the same reasons: beauty, resilience, balm.

The last year of my life has been filled with disappointment, illness, and death. I have always turned toward my gardens when I need comfort, and this year has been no different. It makes sense, in the current context of my life, that my writing would tend toward the memories and lessons I find in soil and soul. Pain and loss are inspirations for seeking meaning.

I have always loved words, sentences, and story. I was what my mother called a "bookworm," and what my friend calls (in her native Spanish) "a girl who eats books." Books are some of my best friends, and reading one of my favorite adventures. It has always been so. The writers who have influenced me are those whose writing is contemplative. Annie Dillard can take me, in just a phrase, to the bank of an icy brook; L.M. Montgomery's "white way of delight" (*Anne of Green Gables*) is a vision that will never leave me; Khalil Gibran's beautiful verses are complimented by his illustrations. I, too, am a contemplative. I write who I am, as all honest writers must.

I garden. That is also part of who I am. When I pound tomato stakes, prune pear trees, mulch beds, or harvest raspberries, I am doing it as a part of the whole. I am a microcosm, in a microcosm, that is part of the macrocosm of all that is. I notice my physical self in this physical space and my spiritual self in this spiritual space; both at once. *Sacred Soil* is a contemplative's short memoir of the hard lessons and comforting reassurances I find as I plan, tend, and toil in my garden.

This collection of memories includes pieces that are overtly about the act of gardening. It contains pieces that are set in the garden but about family dynamics, and it contains pieces for which nothing is peripheral, but all is woven together in a great braid of memory and meaning.

I wrote this collection of pieces in the immediate aftermath of my mother's passing, and in, and after, the times of three other great personal and family losses. I wrote this collection in the dead of a New England winter and the dreariness of a wet spring.

No matter the season or weather, my garden lives its many summers over and over in my memory. In the cold of January, I can conjure up the image of spiraled sunflower seeds ripening in the sun. In the sweetness of every ripe tomato, I can recall the bitterness of blight. I can see October in April and April in October.

I hope that readers will enjoy, and be moved by, these memories, and that they will resonate with the stories of love, and loss, and life in the garden.

—Melina Rudman

1

Haunted Landscape

Like a patient mother,
earth bears our memories in her arms,
carrying in her soil both pain and joy,
silently and without complaint,
until we rise again in glory.

(MARJORY BENNET)

The blackberry thicket is now a haunted place. Soil remembers the imprint of those who tend it, kneel in it, and walk upon it. Some memories are hard and sharp, their energy so heavy that they reverse erosion by making stone from dust, like the dinosaur footprints at a local state park. Others are softer and gentler, like the wondering fingers of a three-year-old as she exposes the moist riches beneath the garden-mulch in her effort to befriend the garden's worm population.

My whole garden, indeed, my home's entire landscape, is imbued with memory, story, and the ghosts of seasons past. There are scars and depressions, growing edges, and bursts of beauty, all owing their present state to the care, or carelessness, of human and non-human beings. This awareness makes me aware of my actions, of my intentions with my life, and the life of home and garden.

My dog, Bailey, will now haunt the soft dirt between green, leafy blackberry canes for as long as they grow there, and the land itself may always be slightly concave where he snuggled and shrugged his little body into the cool earth through all the summer days of his life with me.

Bailey's first visit came at Christmas when he accompanied my daughter home from a Katrina-damaged New Orleans. The little, cocoa-colored, fluffy-furred mutt with black ears and snout was attached to Megan as if by Velcro. He had found her on the fabled Desire Street as she walked to the local corner store, following just far enough behind to be able to run if he needed to, and just close enough so that she would know he was there. At first, he shied away from her and would not eat until she had provided lots of room between herself and the bowl. He slept outside her front door and trotted beside her as she cycled to work each morning, and home again each afternoon. He barked at every person and pet that walked anywhere near the home he was claiming with my daughter.

Finally, in a moment reminiscent of Michael Angelo's Sistine Chapel scene, he allowed Megan to touch his nose with her finger, and the spark of a new life started for them both. Bailey, abandoned by his people before the storm, and Megan, alone and homesick but determined to help the city she loved recover in any way she could, moved in together and became inseparable.

When we flew Meg home for Christmas that year, Bailey came with her. He was skittish with us. While Megan was out visiting a friend, he dashed out of an opened door and ran down the road looking for her, and we all ran after him until we could get him safely home again.

When Megan moved back to Connecticut a few years later with a boyfriend and his giant dog, Hercules, Bailey and Hercules took the twenty-two-hour ride alongside them in the cab of a U-Haul. When the boyfriend and Hercules were no longer part of Megan's life, she moved home with the little dog, and it was Megan and Bailey once again. When Megan married her husband Jeff and moved into his home, it came with a resident cat who did not like dogs. Bailey was content to stay with me, and I was glad to have him.

For five years, Bailey trotted happily beside me wherever I went, the soft tips of his ears bouncing with each step: from room to room, on long walks with our other dogs, and out into the gardens, his toenails clicking on pavement and parquet or sinking into lawn and dirt. He loved the fenced backyard where he could run barking along the property line with the neighbor's dog, roll in the grass (or something stinky), and rummage in compost to his heart's content. Bailey snuffled and snorted, his nose finding the invisible paths of squirrels, chipmunks, and the neighborhood cats who tracked them. He sought out sunshine to warm his bones, and shade to cool his blood, and he often wandered between the two like Goldilocks looking for the bed that was "just right." His favorite spot to relax on hot summer days was the blackberry patch.

Several years ago, I planted five thornless canes at the western edge of my vegetable garden. That first year, one died, but the other four established themselves with roots and leaves. The second year, my neat line of canes filled in with new shoots. By the third year, the canes had become a thicket: tall, wide, trellised, and filled with white flowers and buzzing bees, or juicy, thumb-sized, deep-black berries. Bailey didn't care about the berries; it was the cool and dark he craved, and he claimed the shady cave of canes as his very own.

On days when the sun beat down, and my sweat watered the peppers or tomatoes in big, salty drops, Bailey would be lying quietly in one of the hollows he had scraped out, his brown eyes watching me as I weeded and watered, waiting for me to finish my tasks. He was the most companionable of my dogs; he knew what it was to be alone, and seemed to take it upon himself to be sure I never suffered the same fate. He followed me from place to place and room to room. He slept on my feet at night. Where I was, Bailey was there, too.

Bailey died on a frigid January day in his fifteenth year after suffering a stroke; he will never know another summer day, and I miss him terribly. When spring comes, and the blackberries leaf out, I will peer through the greenery to tell him what a good dog he was.

If the light is just right, I may catch a glimpse of his warm eyes gazing back at me with devotion.

Reflection

Ancient cultures, from Africa to Celtic lands to the Americas' Native peoples, saw the world itself—land, sea, and sky—as alive. Gaia Theory teaches the same thing in contemporary culture. In these times when scientists are discovering what the mystics have always known (which is that Nature has a wisdom all its own, that trees communicate, animals feel, and that everything is not only connected to everything else but is held together in a web of responsive behaviors). Being conscious of these truths, spend a few moments alone in an outdoor spot, experiencing the world *around* you as the world that is *within* you.

Questions for Journaling

- Consider some of your favorite places in Nature— your own garden or yard or a favorite forest trail or beach. What memories are held in these places?

- How does your awareness of these memories affect how you approach and exist in these spaces?
- How will this place remember you when you no longer visit it?

Spirit,
I give thanks
that I am held in a great web of Being,
where the energy of earth and memory,
tree and thought, flower and emotion,
are all knit together
into You.

2

Pruning

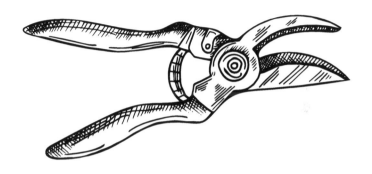

Everything has seasons,
and we have to be able to recognize
when something's time has passed
and be able to move into the next season.
Everything that is alive
requires pruning as well.

(HENRY CLOUD)

*L*ate February is when I prune the grapevines and pear trees with my father. He gifted me with eight tiny vines the first year we owned our home; he died five years later. Still, we choose a bright day in February every year to meet beneath the bare canopy that rests on the split and tilting arms of the arbor, to cut back all the previous year's growth. This year, the bright days have arrived early in the month, and I spent mid-day yesterday peering, snipping, and tugging at the tangled vines that make up the arbor's canopy—and I have the blisters, sore shoulders and whip-marked cheek to prove it.

There is always in February, some one day, at least, when one smells the, yet distant, but surely coming, summer.

(GERTRUDE JEKYLL)

The climate is changing here in central Connecticut giving us wetter winters that fluctuate between extreme cold and unseasonable warmth, and cooler, wetter summers. My Concord grapes, which were first cultivated in Concord, Massachusetts, in 1854, were bred for New England weather, but our weather is not what it used to be. My vines have come down with "black spot," a fungal infection that emerges and spreads in wet weather. The fungus affects the entire plant: vines, foliage, and fruit, leaving the latter shriveled and inedible, and the two former with big, dark splotches. The only cure is to remove all the infected vines and douse new growth with a copper-based fungicide.

My dad's spirit lingers among the grape vines and pear trees he helped me plant. He always took their well-being personally. He did this with everything he loved, and I have inherited the trait. In the garden, he was a mixture of gentleness and ruthlessness; I also inherited the gentleness, but I have to work at being ruthless. "Don't be afraid to cut them way back, honey. Atta girl!" His instructions are repeated every year, though his voice comes through my heart now and not my ears.

This year I am cutting the vines all the way back to the old growth, knowing that I am sacrificing the hope of fruit this year, for a better chance in the future. Once the threat of snow ends, I will carefully rake up all the leaves and litter under the vines before mulching thickly with wood chips. I am hoping that this thick mulch will prevent any fungal spores in the soil from reinfecting the vines. Only time will tell.

The pear trees also need pruning, but I am going to try something new with them. Rather than lopping off branch after branch this winter, I will prune the branches that are unhealthy or rubbing against one another, and leave the major pruning for the summer. I read somewhere that winter pruning encourages trees to grow with abandon, while summer pruning allows them to be more "thoughtful" about it. My pear trees are thirty years old, old for fruit-bearing trees, and I like the idea of thoughtful growth for them—and me.

I turned sixty a month ago and find myself in an incredibly generative time. Growth is more vital when space is made for it, but making space is often painful. Once upon a time, the thick, tangled, blossom-less branches I will lop from the pear trees were supple and covered in flower and fruit. Their tough bark no longer supports such growth, and it is time for them to go so that the new tender branches have air and sunlight. Like my trees, life-branches that are no longer juicy with sap and scent are being pruned away. Old ways of earning money, respect, or prestige no longer feed my heart and soul, and like deadwood, they are cut back and used as compost for the future.

Gardening simply does not allow one to be mentally old, because too many hopes and dreams are yet to be realized.

(ALLAN ARMITAGE)

My dad has been gone for a quarter century, but he lives on in the memory of vine and branch, and in the hearts of his children and grandchildren. He was a humble man who earned his living doing manual labor. He was an artist with words and soil and wood.

When he died in 1994, we scheduled his calling hours from 4:00 to 7:00, as is usual. By 4:30 people were lined up around the room, out the front door of the funeral home, and down the sidewalk. We heard story after story, from teary-eyed people we did not know, about some kindness my father had done for them. My dad was a nobody in circles of power, but the line of people who loved him circled his life and later, the room and funeral home where he lay in repose. It wasn't what my dad did for a living that made people remember him; they remembered who he was: kind, generous, and grateful. This is what they responded to and loved him for.

All of life responds to these things. Pear trees spread when the sun can shine generously through their branches; grape vines respond to loving care. At sixty, my own life is filled with loss and longing, memory and mourning, a strong-but-slowing body and growing spirit. I am like my father in many ways. I am like my pear trees, too. I don't produce as much as I used to, but what I grow now is juicy, sweet, and satisfying.

> *Even as love is for your growth so is he for your pruning.*
>
> **(KHALIL GIBRAN)**

Reflection

All of life responds to loving care; and loving care is a practice of noticing, clearing, inviting, and nurturing those things that give you life. Take four days in the next week and engage with these themes through an "examen" of consciousness. Bring these themes to mind before rising, and then, before retiring for the night, spend some time pondering and/or journaling with these questions:

Day 1: Noticing

Today, what did I notice about the presence and absence of loving care in my life? Who (including myself) loves and cares for me? Who (including myself) withholds love and care from me? In all I did today, when was I practicing loving care, and when was I not?

Day 2: Clearing

Imagine if I were a tree, and my branches were all the many things I am (or feel I am) responsible for. Which branches are healthy, providing me with joy and satisfaction? How can I invest more in these things? Which branches can I name that used to be healthy and joyful, but no longer are? Can I create an ecosystem so that they still are—or is it time to let them go? Which branches are unhealthy, dead, or rubbing against a branch I want to keep? How can I give myself permission to prune these branches from my life?

Day 3: Inviting

Considering who I want to become, what do I need to invite into my life? Be detailed, use your imagination, and write an invitation to those things. Explain why you want them to come into your life.

Day 4: Nurturing

Your invitation(s) have been accepted. Now, what concrete steps do you need to take to be sure they thrive in your life? Do you need to get out of debt, forgive someone (maybe yourself), meditate or pray more? How will you prepare for the life you want?

Spirit,
show me how to participate
in Your loving care for me.
Point out what I need to nurture.
Give me courage to let go of what needs pruning.
Thank You for Your life
flowing through me.

3

Desire and Will

March is the month of expectation,
the things we do not know.

(EMILY DICKINSON)

"Marzo e pazzo" (March is crazy), my father would say every year as the month of his birth arrived. Here in southern New England, a strengthening sun brings me out into the fresh air to survey the snow-battered gardens. March raises hopes and snow-drops, just to dash them again with wind and ice. It feels crazy, indeed. Today our cloudless, windless, warm day is giving way to gray skies. It will snow about a foot here tonight, and then be below freezing all week this first week of the month, before another storm comes in next weekend.

March holds out the promise of spring. My one remaining dog, Ruca, has been walking more slowly these last few days. Not because of her age (though she is thirteen now), but because the top of the earth is slowly thawing and releasing the tantalizing aromas held in cold-storage all winter long. Meanwhile, my granddaughter, who is three, has discovered the joy of getting her boots stuck in the squishy, sucking mud in the backyard. "Mama, I can't move!" she calls with delight. I come to haul her out, and she dashes away to leave muddy boot prints on the snow that still sits in the shadowed corners in the yard.

In March winter is holding back and spring is pulling forward. Something holds and something pulls inside of us too.

(JEAN HERSEY)

I began cutting back the thorn-crowded canes of the black raspberry that has spread from my neighbor's yard to mine. The six-foot branches arc wildly in every direction, like living barbed wire. I have learned to wear leather gloves and pay close attention when handling thorny brambles and rash-inducing vines. Nature is not tame; it is not a respecter of skin, or property lines, or youth, or life itself.

My nephew, Austyn, died last month, six weeks after my mother passed, and one day after his eighteenth birthday. He was undone by the Nature he was a part of; by a microbe, a *Mucor* spore released from a piece of rotting wood or compost, that rose up, and was inhaled by the pale, skinny, boy who had just completed chemotherapy and become cancer-free.

The *Mucor* fungus is "filamentous," or thread-like. Like the invasive black raspberries, once it emerges, it branches out in all directions. It feeds off whatever it lands on: downed branches, rotten apples, immunocompromised humans. If its landing spot is already dead, it breaks it down. When it lands on something alive—and unable to fight it off—its threads kill the host's tissues bit by bit, until life itself ceases. This is what happened to my nephew.

The infection began in Austyn's lung, the same lobe where the soda-can–sized tumor had been discovered eight months earlier. The tumor was a result of lymphoblastic lymphoma. The tumor had been gone for months, shrunk down and disappeared by the medical toxins of his treatment. The fungus took its place. The treatment saved his life, and made him susceptible to death in a new form.

Austyn always reminded me of a summer day: bright and warm. He had hair the color of sunshine and eyes as blue as a July sky. He loved his family, basketball, fishing, and dancing. He was a happy child.

He smiled a lot. He was brave. He was kind. He was my brother's fourth child, the baby of the family (both nuclear and extended). Because of family drama, there was one year when we saw a lot of Austyn, and many years we did not.

I saw him, after a too-long span of several years, when he started chemotherapy, and I didn't see him again until six months later at my mother's memorial service. He was not expected to attend, but he had missed so many things, and he was determined. He came to greet me, and after a short hug, I touched the side of his face lightly with my left hand. He was frail and looked translucent—in the world but no longer quite of it. His eyes were clear. He wore his baseball cap with the bill in back; he had been a bit vain about his beautiful, wavy, thick, hair and didn't want people to see him without it. He also wore a bright red backpack. We didn't get a chance to talk that night. He did not come to the burial the next day; he was exhausted.

Two days later his body temperature spiked to 104 degrees. They rushed him to the hospital and admitted him to Smilow Cancer Center's pediatric ward. They gave him blood and platelets; they gave him medication and care. His parents and siblings surrounded him with love and support. None of it was enough. His breathing became labored, his kidneys shut down, and the fevers raged. Doctors moved him to the Intensive Care Unit, put him into a medically induced coma, and placed him on a respirator. The fungus had found a fertile environment in the young man's body, and it spread beyond lungs and kidneys to spleen, liver, and brain. It began eating through his skin; first one finger, then his top lip, and finally, all across his back. In its mindless pursuance of its own life, it took my nephew like one more downed branch or overripe peach.

March, when days are getting long,
Let thy growing hours be strong to set right some wintry wrong.

(CAROLINE MAY)

Fungi do not choose their environments; they end up where the flow of air or liquid take them. If they can survive and thrive, they do. They are neither good nor evil; such judgements belong to humans alone, though I can say I hated that fungus for the pain it brought.

Last summer I was glad to discover a different fungus, a mycelium mat growing under the mulch around my blueberry bushes. The six blueberries are grouped in a sun-filled raised bed around the rotting stump of a huge Norway maple that came down in a snow storm a few years ago. A "mat" occurs when the threads, or hyphae, become long, overlapping, and intertwined.

Mycelium are vital to the health of soil; they are a vehicle of decomposition, taking wood chips and fallen leaves, and turning them into nutrients. The mycelium, not at all picky about what they eat, are feasting on what is left of the root system of the old maple, and when there is no longer enough matter to host them, they will die, and become food in turn for insects, larvae, and bacteria.

My blueberry bushes struggle for life in the sweet soil of my backyard. They need acidic soil with a high sulphur content to really thrive. My garden, once an apple orchard where cows and sheep were pastured to keep the meadow grasses cropped and fertilize the soil with their manure, is too rich for blueberries—but I love blueberries and am determined to keep trying, so I amend their bed with coffee grounds, wood ash, and sulphur. So far, it has not been enough, and the bushes are spindly and short, with little fruit.

Desire and will, which I have in abundance, aren't always enough to ensure that life will endure. Sometimes the conditions aren't right and cannot be made so. Sometimes life has its own plans. Sometimes what cures us can also kill us. Sometimes we bury our children. Sometimes we stand in silent, sorrowful, support as our brothers bury theirs.

Reflection

I used to believe that my love could change the laws of physics; that it would somehow multiply loaves and fishes if only I were intent enough. I used to believe that my love could protect my loved ones from pain and suffering. I used to believe that love was a force, but that disbelief is a temptation. Now I know that love is only a power; not a power over, not a power to change what is into what I want it to be. Instead, it is a power to create space for what needs to emerge. Only that, and yet, as painful as that can be, that is the power of creation itself.

- What do you desire most?
- What have you believed about the power of your will?
- Have you tried to force change? What has happened?

How do you feel about using the power of love to allow change? What might happen?

*O Life-Giver,
teach me to love as You do,
without condition,
without insisting on my way.
Let my love make room
for whatever needs to come forth,
whether it be dark or light,
sorrow or joy.
Teach me to surrender
to love's true power.*

4

Wilson

Earth, that nourished thee, shall claim
Thy growth, to be resolved to earth again.

(WILLIAM CULLEN BRYANT)

*M*y body started moving before my thoughts coalesced. I sprinted down the fence line where, just moments before, Wilson and Bailey had been running together barking joyously at Riley, who lived on the other side of the fence. The three dogs, Riley on one side, and Wilson and Bailey on the other, had worn a shallow trough along the backyard chain link separating our properties. The barking had changed, though; it had gone from frenzied to ferocious, and I knew what that meant: play had changed to aggression. Wilson had Bailey again.

I stopped just behind Wilson's 125-pound body, planted my feet on either side of his back hips, grabbed the loose skin at the back of his skull with both hands, lifted, and shook. "Wilson! Wilson! Stop it! Stop it!"

Bailey was hanging from Wilson's mouth, curled like a whimpering comma. Wilson, coming back to reality, dropped him, and Bailey took off like a limping shot. I held onto Wilson for a few more minutes. "Bad dog! Bad!" Then I walked him up to the house for a time-out in a closed room.

I came back to find Bailey, frightened and sore, in his spot beneath the blackberry bushes. He was not bleeding, just literally shook up. I patted him and crooned calming words until he stopped trembling, then went inside to check on Wilson, and call my husband.

It was Friday, and my husband Ed, a runner in the first blush of learning he loved to run, was away for the weekend at a road race, this one a relay across Cape Cod. "Honey, we cannot wait any longer. I am going to call the vet." I explained what had happened, then hung up, dialed our veterinarian, and made an appointment for early the next afternoon.

It is a strange thing to know exactly when death will occur; to know that this is a dog's last walk, last dinner, last treat. This knowing brings an uncomfortable anticipation, a desire to notice and remember the amber-color of fur, the incredible softness of ears, the way giant feet sound as they pad across wood floor.

Wilson was never quite right. When we brought the four-month-old Golden Retriever puppy home from the Connecticut Humane Society, we were told that he was inbred. He had a furless circle shaved around each eye which made him look like the negative image of a raccoon. He had needed surgery to repair his eyelids because his lashes had grown inward instead of outward and were scratching his eyeballs. He was huge, goofy, and not very bright. I wanted to name him Lenny after John Steinbeck's character in the novel *Of Mice and Men*, but the puppy was the idea and responsibility of my husband, and he liked the name Wilson.

Nothing retains its form; new shapes from old. Nature, the great inventor, ceaselessly contrives. In all creation, be assured, there is no death—no death, but only change and innovation. . . . death is but to cease to be the same.

(OVID)

By the time Wilson was a year old he had developed idiopathic vestibular disease. Vestibular disease is known by the common name "old dog disease." Wilson was the only yearling our vet had ever seen come down with it. He held his head at a perpetual tilt, he suffered dizzy spells and often walked in circles; he vomited occasionally.

Wilson had cataracts and glaucoma by the time he was eighteen months old. By the time he was two, he needed an eye removed because the pressure behind it was pushing his eyeball forward from his skull. We took him to Massachusetts to see a veterinarian who specializes in eye surgery. She told us that Wilson was a good candidate, but that it would only be a few years before the other eye was affected. She told us how much the surgery would cost, and sent us home to consider our options.

On our drive back to Connecticut, we discussed the dog lying quietly across the back seat behind us. I told Ed it was his decision, that I would support whatever he decided to do, and to be sure (for his own peace of mind) that he made the decision from a loving place.

We stopped in Northampton, Massachusetts, for lunch. Wilson and Ed sat on the patio of a local burger joint while I went in to order.

When I came out with a tray covered in fries and burgers (veggie for me, meat for Ed and Wilson), Ed had made his decision. He had watched as person after person smiled when they saw Wilson sitting quietly beside him. Two weeks later, Wilson had his surgery.

The first night home he cried in pain all night long, and I cried with him. He looked like a monster with his face swollen and his right eyelids stitched together.

I put Wilson on his lead and brought him out into the night-cooled August dark. Walking seemed to soothe him, as if he could out-distance the pain in his face. We walked up and down the sidewalk all night long until dawn came, when Wilson could have another pain pill and fall asleep to continue healing.

Once the swelling went down, Wilson became known around the neighborhood as "the one-eyed dog." His afflictions seemed to bring out the tenderness in people.

Wilson's troubles were not limited to his eyes; he wasn't right in the head, either. Most of the time, almost all of it, he was a good-natured, not-too-smart knucklehead. But there were moments when he was not all right, not by a long-shot. There were moments when Wilson became almost paranoid, when he would look at the other dogs with a malevolent glint in his eye. We began to watch Wilson closely, ready to step in. Wilson was never violent with a human, but his neurological troubles frightened my frail, aged mother, and worried me and Ed.

As his eyesight grew dimmer, the shadows in Wilson's mind seemed to grow stronger, and he became more and more unpredictable with our other dogs, Bailey and Ruca. Ed and I began to talk about euthanasia. We talked about it, but ending a life is a terrible responsibility, and so talk didn't become action until Wilson's behavior made the decision for us.

"Wilson! Come on, let's go for a ride." I buckled his leash and led him to the car, where he jumped obligingly into the back seat. I drove to Cromwell with tears in my eyes while Wilson hung his head out the window, floppy ears blowing in the wind. We were led into an examination room.

One of the group's veterinarians, someone we had not met yet, came in to talk with me. I wondered whether she was trying to talk me out of the decision. I told her all about Wilson: the eyes, the vestibular disease, the aggression and violence. She talked about how difficult it would be to "re-home" a dog like Wilson. She talked about specialists. I listened, and gave the same response again and again: "We love him. He is dangerous. I don't want him to be afraid, I don't want him to feel abandoned, I don't want him to suffer, and I don't want my other dogs, or any person, to be hurt by him."

She left the room and then came back. "Does he greet you at the door when you come home?" I was puzzled, but answered her question. "No. No, he never has." She nodded and left the room again.

My response must have satisfied her somehow because, when she returned again, she was finally ready to talk about what I had come there to do: kill my own dog. Wilson was anxious by then, and I was heartbroken. They brought in a soft blanket for him to lie on and explained that they would give him a shot to make him sleepy, and then another to stop his heart. They asked me whether I wanted his remains shipped to me after cremation ("no"); they brought the paperwork and billing in so I could just leave afterwards.

"Do you want to stay with him through the process?"
"Yes."

I stroked Wilson's soft fur and told him I loved him as his eyelids fluttered and his heart stilled. I wept alone on the white tile floor while his body relaxed and cooled. I drove home to tell Ruca and Bailey that they were safe now. I had done the right, and terrible, thing. When Ed called after his race and heard my tear-choked voice, he said he should have been there.

The earth on both sides of the old metal fence is still worn smooth and lifeless from the feet of the three dogs who pounded it almost to stone. In heavy rains, the water runs over the compressed ground like a tiny stream in torrent until it reaches a clump of purple lilacs, where it soaks into soil that is soft and filled with the pill bugs and earthworms that munch on death and defecate life.

If you really want to draw close to your garden, you must remember first of all that you are dealing with a being that lives and dies; like the human body, with its poor flesh, its illnesses at times repugnant.

(FERNAND LEQUENNE)

Reflection

In this essay I say that I had done "the right and terrible thing." When have you been faced with a decision where the right thing to do is also the thing you do not want to do? What did you learn about yourself as you leaned into, and then lived into, your decision? How does Nature, and your spirituality, inform your decision-making process?

The soil continually reminds me that life and death are intertwined, one feeding into the other. Does this comfort you—or cause you sorrow? Is there room in our hearts, do you think, for both comfort *and* sorrow? For love that is both "terrible" and yet generously "right"?

Lover-of-Life,
do You weep over Your fallen creatures,
even as You gather them in
to Yourself?

5

Lilacs and Turtles

One must not count the losses,
they would be too alarming.
One must count only the joys,
and feel continually blessed in them.

(MAY SARTON)

I had a new baby, one I had adopted from out of state. She was not strong or vital, but she held out the promise of a long, fragrant life if I could give her a sheltered place to flourish. The new baby was a common lilac, her name *syringa vulgaris*, her three branches each about twelve inches tall. This particular plant had been bred for the pale white flowers that made her more fragile than her cousins of the purple variety. I found her at a roadside nursery in southern Maine on a short trip north to visit friends.

When we got home, I carried her to the backyard to be planted near the northeast corner of our house. I had chosen a site where our home would shelter the young plant from the worst of the winter winds, as well as the burning sun of summer. I had visions of opening the living room window as her perfume wafted in on warm spring breezes. I showed her new home to my husband (who is not a lover of plants and gardens), so he wouldn't mow her over while cutting the lawn, as he had done with other plants. I spent the next two weeks being sure she had what was needed to survive transplant and begin growing her roots deep into the warm soil. The young tree put out new leaves and settled into life, and I stopped hovering.

Weeks later, I walked out of the back door and began my nightly circuit of the gardens. My feet were bare and our dogs, still young then, frolicked beside me. Going counter-clockwise brought me down the long stretch of fence to the vegetable beds, pears, and grapes, before coming back up the opposite long border toward the back of the house. All was as it should be.

When I got to the lilac's home, I bent to run my hands through the lilac's foliage, but they found nothing but air. The tree had disappeared. I stepped back to get my bearings, and bent again to where the plant should have been. There was nothing there except three, short sticks, their tops shredded and torn.

I straightened up as realization dawned. It had happened again. My solar plexus went cold. I walked back into the house, through the kitchen, and up the stairs. My husband was watching the Atlanta Braves baseball team win or lose again. I turned the television off and asked, "Did you cut the grass yesterday?"

My tone tipped him off; when I get angry my voice gets soft and as still as a coating of ice on a winter stream. He nodded slowly.

"Would you come with me please?" He sighed, stood, and walked behind me, a man being led to his reckoning.

When we got to the crime scene, I pointed to the three little sticks. "What is supposed to be there?" My voice was dripping with calm.

"Where? What?" He knew he was in trouble but still had no idea why.

His not-knowing did it; adrenaline coursed through me and the ice broke up to be replaced by molten rock, as my fury coursed up, and out. I bent from the waist, wrapped my right hand around the three sticks and pulled. The entire root ball lifted from the earth and I held it above my head like Thor with his hammer. I waved the sticks and soil in the air, as if they were weightless, punctuating my words with movement.

"I showed you where this tree was! I showed you and you killed it with the lawnmower! Don't you ever listen to me?" My voice rose as the potting soil showered down on my head, and my husband stood, mute and amazed, at the crazed and aggrieved mother of a murdered lilac who raged in front of him. I ran out of words before I ran out of anger, and he took advantage of the quiet to escape back into the relative safety of the house and ballgame. I sat near the hole in the earth where the little tree had lived its short life, and I wept. I wept for the little tree, and for the future it would not have.

I weep often over the ways our human carelessness affects the world around us. We mow our lawns in straight lines and don't notice rabbit nests, seedlings, or the bees in the clover. We remove every living thing from land before building homes, and then attempt to replace an ecosystem with lonely trees, lawn, and neatly carved shrubbery. I notice this carelessness most often when I am driving. We strap ourselves into speeding metal boxes and proceed to move from point A to point B without a thought of the roads that run through neighborhoods, meadows, and forests, and the life contained in each.

Several years ago I came across a huge, old, snapping turtle crossing a busy road. It was spring, and the birds and the bees were not the only creatures interested in procreation. I stopped my car, and then stopped traffic, an unauthorized Nature-cop. Cars had lined up in both directions; some drivers smiled and others scowled as the turtle plodded along. A young woman got out of a car, jogged up to the turtle, stood behind it, placed her hands just-so, and carried it to the side of the road.

"How did you know where to lift it safely?" I asked.

She smiled and said proudly, "I work at Petco."

I told her she was a hero.

A couple of years later, after a long day at a job that wore on me, I came across a much smaller turtle making its way across another, quieter road. I thought about stopping, but dinner was waiting at home, and I kept going, hoping it would be safe. I got about half a mile away, worried all the time, before I turned back to do what I should have done immediately.

In the two minutes between my decision to keep going, and my decision to turn back, the little turtle had been run over, its shell crushed, its innards seeping out onto the road.

Years later, my eyes still move to the accident-scene every time I drive that road, and I apologize to God and the spirit of that little turtle that lost its precious life to someone who didn't see it and swerve, and someone who did see it and kept going.

"Wake up!" my garden cried this morning. "Wake up and see me today, see me now, this instant, for I can make no promises about tomorrow. The wind may strip my blossoms, the worm may eat my fruit, but today, this moment, I am here, full, replete. Come see 'fore 'tis all gone!"

(ALICE DIBELL)

It seems that wherever time-economy and speed are prioritized over life and mindfulness, Nature suffers. The garden has taught me to slow down, to see life, death, danger, and opportunity. My garden is always in the present moment, and it shows me, again and again, that the present moment is the only time I really have.

Reflection

I recently saw a photo on social media of a young deer standing in the middle of a two-lane road. The caption asked that we not see a deer crossing the road, but a road cutting through the deer's forest home. Take a long, contemplative "look" at your home and its ecosystems. Where does human convenience compromise the lives of other creatures? Let yourself have feelings about this; notice what those feelings are. How might you become more aware of the lives around your life? What have you seen for so long that you no longer see it? What sounds do you no longer hear? When does your busy-ness overrun your kindness? What is your best mindfulness practice to counter this?

Spirit, Earth,
I ask Your pardon
for all the ways I've hurt Your life.
Teach me to be more aware.
Show me how to live
in harmony with You
and all Your creatures.

6

Bearded Iris

This, this! Is Beauty. Cast,
I pray, your eyes
On this my Glory!
See the Grace, the Size!

(GEORGE CRABBE)

I was about ten years old when I saw my first blue and gold miracle. *Iris germanica*. Bearded iris.

There are moments and experiences from my life that are as clear in my mind as the moment they happened. That single, pale blue bloom on a thick stem above spear-shaped leaves is one of those experiences. I can "see" my ten-year-old self in blue cotton shorts, pink tee shirt, and white cotton sneakers with rubber covering the toes, standing beside the front steps of a friend's dark brown house, so captivated by a flower that I forgot to knock on the door.

I got very close to that flower. It had three upward-facing petals (which I now know are called "standards,") and three downward facing petals (called "falls.") I touched the soft, golden-yellow of the "beard" that grew on the falls and drew away an index finger covered in pollen. I bent my nose to the flower's center and inhaled the scent of heaven: light, sweet, unlike anything else I have ever found. I am not sure how long I stood enraptured before my friend Trudy, who was expecting me, came outside, and together we ran across the street to the little wooded plot to build a fort among the raspberry brambles.

Years later, I drive by that house occasionally, and I always glance to the same spot where the iris still blooms in my memory, its beauty capturing the imagination of a child.

Light-blue bearded iris now line the walkway from my front door to driveway, and every day of their yearly bloom in June, I stop and bury my nose deep in the cup of their blossoms, as though I were some sort of flower-sommelier. They still smell like heaven.

The iris share their space with hydrangea, salvia, coreopsis, evening primrose, black-eyed Susan, purple coneflowers, garlic chives, sedum, and bachelors' buttons. Walk down the cobbled pavers in late June or early July, and you will find yourself in a swirl of color, scent, and sound, as plants bloom, perfume rises into the warm air, and bees buzz and bustle among the flowers. I live in the midst of miracles. I do this on purpose.

My first teacher in the garden was my father, and he learned how to grow things from his own father. I did not learn about flowers, though, from either of them. Flowers were something I learned straight from Nature.

My father's parents, Giuseppe Salafia and Carmelina Carta, both emigrated to Middletown, Connecticut, from its "sister city" Melilli, a tiny town on the southeast coast of Sicily. My grandfather came alone as a very young man and lived with his brothers, who were already here. My grandmother, still a child, came with her parents. Giuseppe and Carmelina met and married here.

In Sicily, the Salafia family was very poor, while the Cartas were more affluent, though "affluence" is a perspective of time and place. The Salafias eked out a living fishing, growing vegetables, and tending sheep. Young Giuseppe left school after third grade and was sent into the mountains, alone, as a shepherd for his family's small flock. He was eight years old. His mother, Giuseppina, packed bread, cheese, and dried fish for him, and one of his fifteen siblings would hike up to the pasture-land every three days to bring him fresh supplies. He learned to trap rabbits and then wring their necks, skin, and roast them over a scrub fire; he learned what plants he could and could not eat. He learned to protect the sheep and lambs. He learned that life was hard, and food was sometimes a luxury.

When my grandfather bought his own home here in the States and moved his young family into the house on Bidwell Terrace in Middletown, he purchased a cow for milk, and he planted pear, plum, and apple trees. He grew tomatoes and jarred their sauce. He grew peppers that he roasted on an outside fire before rubbing the blackened skin from them and preserving them in lemon juice and olive oil for pepper and egg sandwiches, made with the thick, crusty bread my grandmother baked every Wednesday. He did all of this while working full time making men's suspenders at the Russell Company mills down the street. He used every bit of space to grow food, and yet his five children sometimes went to bed hungry; it was the time of the Great Depression, and the Salafia family was still poor.

My father remembered that hunger, and its antidote, all his life. He recalled his soft-hearted mother crying every spring as the new calf was taken from its protesting mother to become veal sausage, which she refused to eat. He thought about his father making sun-dried tomatoes on old window screens that had been scrubbed with an iron brush and sterilized with boiling water. He remembered clearing the cow shed and spreading manure and straw around the fruit trees and in the vegetable garden to boost yield. He knew the feeling of wealth when the family could afford a piece of chicken or rabbit on Sundays. He remembered his aunts using hardboiled eggs to provide some protein for the Christmas lasagna.

He remembered all these lessons of his childhood when, a grown man and father of two, he moved our family from Middletown to Cromwell, Connecticut, in 1973. The house we moved from was small, neat, and new, with a postage-stamp–sized yard. The house we moved to, an 1850s farmhouse, was larger, dilapidated, and outdated; but it had a huge yard and an old barn and lean-to.

My mother hated that house. It was cold, drafty, and dusty, and when we moved in, every room in the house was painted dark blue. Four years before we bought it, the house had been purchased by a young couple with newborn twin girls. When those babies were two, their father had drowned in a boating accident on the Connecticut River. In her grief, his young widow had painted the house to reflect her state of mind. My mother set to work with a brush, roller, and white paint almost immediately.

As much as my mother hated that house, my father loved it. He loved the possibilities and potential of it. Mostly, he loved the yard with its own small woodlot at the top of the westward hill, which sloped down gently to the house and outbuildings, all of which were nestled under the spreading branches of an immense, old sugar maple.

Within a year or two, my father had planted a small orchard of peach, plum, and apple trees below the woodlot. He had a large grape arbor to the south of the trees and a huge vegetable garden at the base of this hill where the sun shone all day.

He did not plant flowers. When my mother dared to plant a rose bush beneath the dining room window one warm June day in my fifteenth year, he begrudged her the space. I had seldom seen any tension between them, but that red rose bush caused him to shake his head in disapproval, while she set her chin in determination. The need to provide sang in his blood, and while we put up bushels of peppers, tomatoes, corn, and broccoli, we never had a vase of home-grown flowers on the table; my father didn't see the point in having them.

When I showed my own home to my father years after his health failed, and my parents had moved to an apartment to spare him from shoveling and raking, his first comment was, "Honey, what a garden we could have in this backyard!" He was right about that, though my garden does not look at all like his did, with its straight lines of peppers and tomatoes growing in military formation, where nothing ever bloomed except fruit trees and vegetables.

My vegetable garden is lush and curvy; it's a feminist's garden. Perennials like rhubarb, asparagus, chives, and horseradish grow in clumps instead of rows. Calendula, borage, and dill self-seed each year, and I am content to let them grow where they choose. I am looser with "rules" than my dad was, but I am every bit as serious about the garden.

A few summers ago I noticed that my summer squash and zucchini plants were getting sick just after producing their first, glossy, tender, delicious fruits. One by one, the giant, green, umbrella-shaped leaves began to droop, then wither, until the plants gave up their ghosts and died. I poked around under the leaves and found scads of prehistoric-looking, dark gray insects swarming on the underside of the leaves and scrabbling through the soil beneath the plants: squash bugs.

Anasa tristis finds everything it needs for life in one plant family: the cucurbits, which include squash (both summer and winter,) pumpkins, and cucumbers. They will eat winter squash and cucumbers, but they *love* summer squash. Sometime in the middle of June, females lay their copper-colored eggs on the underside of the plants' leaves just where the veins form a V. Nymphs hatch from the eggs about ten days later, and within four to six weeks, they mature into fast-moving, sap-sucking, voracious killers of the *Costata romanesco* (a delicious Italian heirloom) and crookneck squash that I have babied since they were seedlings. Both the nymphs and the adults pierce the tender stems of the plant to drink its life from it. Their saliva is toxic to the plants, and the puncture wounds never fully heal. The plants weaken, bit by bit and bite by bite, until they lay down their leaves and die. It infuriates me.

I spent days that first summer of the invasion poking around the plants armed with a bucket of soapy water, scraping eggs and throwing the crawly adults into the suds to drown among the bubbles. I hated doing it. I don't end the lives of other creatures easily or without conscience. I know that somewhere in the grand scheme of Nature there is a necessary niche for these bugs that I consider vampire-assassin pests. I refuse to use poisons in my gardens, and for a few years I lost all my squash to their appetites.

Then, one day two winters ago, I read that squash bugs do not like nasturtiums, but nasturtium and squash love each other. I had my answer. That summer I made sure I planted my squash and cucumbers in rich compost, and I surrounded them with nasturtiums.

Nasturtium (*Tropaeolum majus*) are one of my favorite annuals. They have bright orange and yellow flowers and breeze-fluttering, disc-shaped leaves. They grow low to the ground on long stems that push their foliage and flowers into whatever sunlight they can find. Nasturtium are edible plants, leaves and flowers adding a bright, peppery flavor to summer salads.

Each spring, the hard seeds must be soaked in water for several hours before planting. After their hard-entry into the world, they grow with a tender ease everywhere in my gardens. I still have squash bugs, but not as many. I don't begrudge them their lives if they don't kill my plants. The nasturtium discourage enough of the squash-bugs so that they can eat, and so can I.

These days I plant many flowering annuals in my vegetable beds. Cosmos wave their pink petals above the compact, yellow and orange variegated marigolds that line the garden's wheelbarrow path. Bronze fennel, with its light green umbrels and dusky feathered foliage, flutters between lettuce and broccoli. Annual black-eyed Susans (*Rudbeckia hirta*) with their bright flowers and fuzzy leaves are little splashes of sunshine ringing the gray-green leaves of eggplant.

Interplanting, or companion planting, mimics Nature in her design of ecosystems. Before they were domesticated, apple and almond trees did not grow in pruned rows of thousands. Tomatoes, which are actually vines, twirled and twined themselves across the ground and around whatever they could find. Fruit-bearing plants and tender edible leaves like lettuces and cress were part of meadows and wetlands that were filled with birds, bugs, and bees. I create a bit of that ecosystem in my own gardens where apple, chestnut, cherry, and pear trees are interspersed with grapevines, elderberry, raspberries, sunflowers, and Queen Anne's lace. All of this diversity brings bumble, green, ground, and honey bees; mantids; hornworms; squash bugs; and cabbage moths. It brings the birds and wasps that munch on the insects, and it brings the occasional brave bunny and nighttime skunk.

What would the world be, once bereft Of wet and wildness? Let them be left, O let them be left, wildness and wet; Long live the weeds and the wilderness yet.

(GERARD MANLEY HOPKINS)

In the front yard, ferns and hosta frame my home's foundation. Purple *Buddleia* (butterfly bush), which smells as sweet as cotton candy tastes, and prickly blue globe thistle bring skippers, painted lady, and black swallowtail butterflies. The purple coneflowers attract bees and, once the seed matures in August, gold finches that flit and feast on the bobbing heads.

Flowers and fruit feed my soul. They bring beauty and vitality to what was once an expanse of lifeless lawn. My gardens are my own little slices of Eden, places for life to emerge. My blood sings with the need to provide not just for my family and friends, but for Nature itself, of which I am the tiniest part for this one moment in time.

In good years, my father and his ancestors were subsistence gardeners, growing enough for their families but with nothing extra for selling or sharing. There was never really enough time or space to grow anything that did not contribute to the dinner table. Beauty was saved for church, and their eyes were focused on survival. I, however, have been fortunate to live in a place and time where food is plentiful, and where beauty is not superfluous but necessary. My family is not poor, and we are surrounded by flowers from April through October.

Reflection

Infants and young children notice everything. As we grow, we pick up messages (some spoken, some unspoken, some about survival itself) about what we ought to focus on, and most of us forget the scents and sounds of childhood, such as the way the air smells just after it rains. We get rewarded for "keeping our eyes on the prize," and we miss seeing the beauty of the roadside. Remembering to notice and discerning what is actually vital (as opposed to what I have been told is vital) has been one of the spiritual practices of my life. It is a practice that can form from asking these questions:

- What are the photographic memories of your life?
- How does the past (ancestral and immediate) inform your present?
- Where do you find beauty? Where is it in the hierarchy of your needs?
- What have you stopped noticing? What do you want to notice again?
- What miracles do you dwell in? (Hint: it is all miracle!)

Spirit of Beauty,
teach me to always see Your face.
Spirit of Kindness,
tug at my heart.
May I never be too busy to heed Your call.

7

Cycles

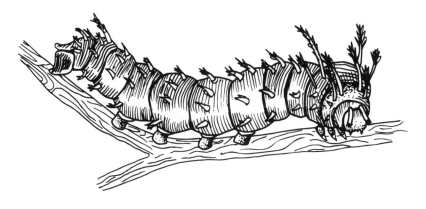

*There is an appointed time for everything.
And there is a time
for every event under heaven -
A time to give birth, and a time to die;
A time to plant and a time
to uproot what is planted.*

(ECCLESIASTES, 3:1–2)

The sight startled me and made me drop my basket, cherry tomatoes spilling out into the sweet-smelling straw I use for mulch. I stepped back a few paces to compose myself, then reached to turn the leaf over and peer again at the monster.

Yep, still there: as long as my pinky finger and twice as fat, light green except for the strange, white, tumor-type things, sticking out all over it. I had to Google it on my phone before I knew what it was: a tomato hornworm who was short on time. The "tumors" were parasitic wasp eggs that would soon hatch and eat the caterpillar from the inside out. It made me a bit squeamish. I wouldn't wish such an end on any creature, not even a tomato hornworm.

As a child, I remember watching my grandfather heal a little peach tree. My father had planted it several years earlier and it had done well, but that particular summer it seemed to be giving up the ghost, and my father knew he needed the help of an expert to save it. My grandfather came to our house one day like an old-time medical doctor making a house call. He approached the tree with care and respect, the way one approaches any wild thing that is fighting for its life. He walked up to and around it, slowly, gently, almost as if he were trying not to frighten it. When he touched the tree, it was like a caress, his calloused, sensitive hands fluttering through the straggly leaves and stroking its bark.

At the base of the tree, just above the grass-line, he discovered a tiny, sap-seeping hole bored into the trunk. "Melina, bring me a wire hanger," he said in his thick, accented English. When I handed it to him he unwound the wire, knelt in the grass, and began threading the wire up, up, into the tree. After several minutes, he nodded to himself, and drew the wire out. There, skewered at its end, a small worm wriggled in its death throes. The tree recovered, my father rejoiced, and we all ate peaches.

My garden is one of my greatest teachers. When I approach it with respect and care, it returns the favor; when I honor its systems, it welcomes me into them. Its lessons, both beautiful and gory, are profound. Through the doomed worms, I realized that life consumes death in the garden. My grandfather killed the worm so that we could eat peaches, and Nature follows the same merciless rhythm: wasp larvae eat caterpillars alive; mantids, untroubled by conscience, munch on bumble-bees; fungi feast on decomposing wood; pepper plants draw the nutrients of their ancestors out of the compost to set fruit of their own. Death does not end life, it feeds it.

July is the soul of summer in New England. Long hot days, and nights soft and warm as lambswool follow one another without haste or worry. Only the occasional thunderstorm with gusty winds and fat, heavy raindrops breaks the hold of the sun, and quenches the thirst of plants and creatures alike.

Follow the path into my summer garden and you will see blackberries arching, grapevines grasping, pears swelling, lettuce bolting, raspberries invading, and sunflowers, calendula, and borage abuzz with bees. July is the crescendo of the summer garden, all the other months are either preparation for, or recovery from, the life energy of July.

Where I live, spring starts slowly before exploding with life: birds, bugs, and blueberry bushes singing, humming, and flowering in a frenzy of courtship and sex. Spring is when I feed the soil and prepare the garden for planting. Only the most hardy of plants like peas and lettuce take root and thrive before mid-April finally warms the Connecticut air.

By mid-September, the last blackberries have been picked and the tomatoes lose their sweetness, the basil is bitter, and any pears still unharvested are alive with wasps intoxicated by their sugary flesh. Autumn is a time to clean and clear, to harvest fall crops and apply the next thick coat of mulch to blanket the soil so that winter's chill won't break it open like the split-skin of chapped knuckles.

Nothing is permanent but change.

(HERACLITUS)

July, though, seems at once eternal and fleeting, urgent and laid-back. July is when birds are fledging, tomatoes are blushing ,and eggplants form like purple tears. For just a day or two in July, summer is perfectly balanced between the growth of spring and the ripening of autumn—and then the Earth shifts, and everything changes.

If ever I find myself clinging to an old way of being, I need only step outside to be reminded that change is constant. The garden is never static; it moves from desolation to verdancy, from verdancy to abundance, and from abundance to death and decomposition before returning to rest during our long Connecticut winters.

It changes minute by minute, day by day, and year by year; enlarging, maturing, contracting and shifting; just like me, just like you, just like us. Life is eternal, but our lives are only a moment.

Thirty-five years ago, the African violets on my grandmother's table began to die. She had had a thriving "garden" of them along her east-facing window for twelve years, since my dominating grandfather had passed away, leaving her

Who forces time is pushed back by time; who yields to time finds time a friend.

(THE TALMUD)

the freedom to have a life of her own. By the time she entered the nursing home where she would live out her final year, they were gone, despite the care she still lavished on them.

In the last few years, I noticed the same thing happening with the plants that wintered in my mother's favorite room. The spider plants and pothos seem to hover somewhere between life and death, just like my frail, ninety-year-old mother had. When I moved them to another room, they gained vibrancy again.

I notice now the connections between my own health and well-being and the health and well-being of the life in and around me. My plants tell me when I am low on energy, when I need to rest and recoup. As I age, I trust that they will let me know when it is time to let go, and do less.

In thirty years, my garden and I have become woven together, our life energies intertwined and interdependent. It is a lover, spiritual director, teacher, partner, and friend. I know peace when working its soil, I see the Divine in its life, I feel joy when a bee uses me as a resting spot, or when I notice the red shoulders of rhubarb first shrugging themselves out of the cold earth.

Life is a force that waxes and wanes, ebbs and flows. All of life responds to the energy in all of life. It affects and infects potted plants and human beings. We may call it "spring fever," "summer love," "hibernation," or "seasonal affective disorder," but we are in it, and it is in us.

And as I tend the garden, it tends me. I plant potatoes and harvest patience, sow spinach and reap serenity, add compost and humous to the soil and remember that I, too, am dust, and that, someday, my body will go back to the earth, my death feeding new life in the way of all things forever and ever. Amen.

Reflection

We are all subject to the seasons and the laws of life: gestation, birth, life, aging, death. What falls into the earth and dies is reborn in the dark and emerges as new life. What we grow in the shadows, produces fruit in the light.

- What patterns in Nature speak most to you?
- What are your beliefs about control and change?
- Do you connect the word *change* with death—or birth? Or both?

Spirit,
may I learn the lessons
the Earth teaches me—
may I learn to surrender to change,
to death,
and to new birth.

8

Love and Connection

The glory of gardening:
hands in the dirt,
head in the sun,
heart with nature.
To nurture a garden is to feed
not just the body, but the soul.

(ALFRED AUSTIN)

Gardening is in my DNA the way the Earth's minerals are in my bones and blood. Calcium, iron, and copper, the trace ingredients of life; and soil, water, sun, and seed, the building blocks of soul. My father inherited his love of growing things from my Sicilian grandfather whose garden was legendary in the family, and I inherited my own love from my father. My mother's Irish mother had "green hands" that would bring even the most fragile things back to robust health if it were within the laws of Nature. For the years my grandmother was well and lived with my family, she and my father were unstoppable in the garden, hauling in bushels of squash, peppers, tomatoes, and broccoli that needed to be blanched and frozen to sustain us through the cold months. Growth, healing, and food are as much a part of my family tree as the cool green fields of Ireland and the sunbaked volcanic soil of Sicily.

I am a gardener for the same reasons I am a lover and a writer; it is who I am and there is no escaping it. In the years that busyness pulls me away from my own backyard and I see how the wild plants have taken over the herb garden or the grapes have gone mostly to the birds before I could harvest them, I think about taking a year off, or scaling the garden way back. It would be the logical, practical, thing to do—and the idea is utterly joyless. Instead, as the year turns, so does my mindset. I turn the pages of the seed and plant catalogs that burst from my mailbox and dream of creamy purple potatoes and pink raspberries, nodding nasturtiums and weedless rows.

Love is the energy of creation. Anyone can learn the skills of gardening but if you don't love it, don't do it. For life to thrive it must be loved; this is true of human beings, chimpanzees, cheetahs, orchards, and broccoli rabe.

When I first began growing things in the long yard behind my home, it was a struggle. The previous owner had been a "lawnaholic;" a compulsive mower and fertilizer. His actions drained the soil of life; no worms, no bugs, nary a dandelion nor plantain in the perfect green carpet that stretched from my backdoor to the neighbor's fence. That yard is more garden than lawn these days; more mosaic that monochrome. Most of the grass has been converted to beds, and what little remaining fescue is left is patchy, sparse, and well-trodden by people and dogs. The beds, though, are lush and living, providing life from root to fruit for themselves, my family and friends, the bees, firebugs, and butterflies.

I used to try to control the garden, to have neat rows of properly staked tomatoes with nothing but bare soil between the plants. This never worked. Inevitably, under the hot sun of late June and July (when the heat would chase me from the garden by eleven o'clock each morning), the bare soil would provide the perfect spot for weed after weed to pop up and overtake my plot, and I would end my summer sore, tired, and discouraged.

One night several years ago, after a long, frustrating day wrestling with the weeds that were choking out my asparagus bed, I dreamed I was standing naked in the garden under a full moon. The air was moist and warm, the night quiet, as if it were waiting for something. I stood still and gazed about—and realized how much I loved it all, everything from the ragweed and rhubarb to the curly dock, cucumbers, and cabbage moths. At that point my fingers and toes began to tingle. I looked to see tender-green foliage sprouting from my fingertips while my toes spread like roots into the soil.

That dream changed my life, and the garden's life too. I hung my hoe in the shed, put down my preconceived ideas, and began loving the entire thing for itself, not just the fruits that grew from it. I entered into a new relationship with my land, an understanding that it does not belong to me in any way except the legal way human beings title property. It is alive, it is determined, it belongs to itself, and I could either continue to battle with it—or I could listen to it and facilitate its growth.

In nature we never see anything isolated, but everything in connection with something else which is before it, beside it, under it and over it.

(JOHANN WOLFGANG VON GOETHE)

Once I decided to listen, I realized how intertwined I was with the natural world and its processes. I began to understand the needs of the trees, the songs of the birds, the work of the worms. I made space for life, and life filled that space without hesitation: trees, tomatoes, snap peas, and soil.

My work in the garden has taught me that everything is connected, everything is one thing. When we

damage anything with our words or actions (from kill-
ing a spider, to clear-cutting a forest, or supporting factory farming), we damage everything. When we heal
anything (from creating habitat for insects and birds, to
composting, being kind to our neighbors, and supporting small, local farms), we heal everything.

Reflection

Many ancient cultures have revered the symbol of the Tree
of Life; my favorite image of this is a tree enclosed within a
circle, its branches and roots perfect mirrors of each other:
one above ground and visible, the other below ground and
hidden. "As above, so below. As within, so without."

We are each a tree of life. We live upon a small,
blue and green planet within a thin and fragile atmospheric
bubble. Our branches are interwoven.

- Name some of the "branches" of your life. How do
  they give life to and receive life from others?
- What are some of your greatest teachers, and what
  have you learned from them? (Remember, sometimes
  we learn things that are not true.)
- What lesson might Nature be wanting you to learn at
  this phase of your life?

Spirit of the Cosmos,
I ask that you give me healing hands.
May each thing I do
contribute to Your life.
And may each thing I do
open me wider
to Your healing,
Your teaching.

9

Half Seasons

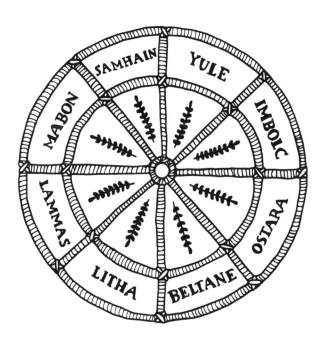

In the springtime,
leaves unfolding,
Growing, growing one by one,
In the summer, always giving
Cool, green shade to every one;
In the autumn, tall and stately,
Dressed in yellow, red and brown,

In the winter, sleeping, sleeping,
While the snow comes softly down.

(CHARLOTTE LAY DEWEY)

Megan was one of those children whose every mood was painted vividly upon her face and in her eyes. When she was happy, she sparkled: eyes shining, smile wide, joy visible. When she was sad, huge tears pooled in her brown eyes before tracing their way down her face to drip from chin to chest. If she were hurt, she howled. If she were angry, she fought. She never walked carefully or sedately; she either careened and catapulted from one place to another or dragged her feet while voicing some protest. Megan is my middle-child, but there has never been anything half-way or moderate about her. Today, Meg is an artist, a creative healer, helper, and defender.

When she was little, her individuality, fashion sense, and artistry developed early. From first grade on, she refused to wear socks that matched; she wore big, flowery "church-hats" to elementary school, mixing patterns and colors the way she mixed paint. She wore every necklace she owned all at once, and piled barrettes and hairbands on top of one another. The idea that "less is more" escaped her.

Meg was also often lonely. She was kind, but she was different, and she was often left out of things by girls whose power came from fitting in, who demanded that their friends do the same. She spent a lot of time at home alone: reading, painting, playing with her toys and her little sister.

One rainy summer morning just after her tenth birthday I found Megan standing on a step stool in front of the mirror in my bathroom. Her cheeks glowed with perfectly-round, rose-colored circles of blush. Her lips were stained deep red, and she had turned her attention to her eyelids and lashes with my small tray of eyeshadow and mascara. I hid my smile, knowing that I was seeing the wonderful and tender Norman Rockwell painting, *Girl at the Mirror*, play out in my very own house, with my own child.

We had a brief conversation about not wearing makeup outside the house until she was older, and then I left so she could complete her toilette as I finished the laundry and tidied the house. I made my way from washing machine, to clothesline, to dining room, and back to the kitchen to scrub the sink, which sits below a window facing into the backyard.

I look out that window every day of the year as the sunrise moves from southeast to due east, to northeast, and back again, in the eternal dance of equinoxes and solstices. Standing warm in my kitchen, I watch the snow fall and cover the yard, I see how the patterns of melt and freeze dimple the ground in early spring, and how the maple leaves cover the green grass as they fall in drifts of gold and red each autumn.

From that window, I watched my children play on the tire swing that hung from the strong branches of a Norway maple that dominated my backyard for most of my years here until, nine years ago, an October snowstorm broke off all the tree's leaf-laden branches in one terrible night of cracks and booms.

But that particular year of my daughter's life, the year she decide to use my makeup, the tree was still vital and strong, and the tire still swung back and forth on its long, thick rope in response to wind and children's play. Beneath the swing, the ground had been eroded by hundreds of little footsteps scuffing across it, until there was a shallow dip that collected snowmelt and rainwater.

That particular late-July day, when my daughter was poised on the cusp between childhood and young womanhood, the morning rain had given way to clear skies and warm breezes. I heard Meg walk behind me out the back door into the yard, and I smiled to myself, glad she had moved on to a new form of entertainment. I finished cleaning, then looked up—and froze, my gaze on something holy.

My daughter, with her glowing cheeks, red lips, and purple eyes, was crouched barefooted beside the tire swing, busily making mud pies in cast-off kitchen ware. She wore mud to her ankles and elbows, like a pair of tight brown socks and opera gloves. All her attention was focused on the dark water, slippery muck, and white clover she was using to decorate her creations.

It was a sacred moment, and I knew it, and I remember it as such. My daughter was in liminal space: the space between childhood and young adulthood. That space was fluid, like Nature itself, and Meg moved easily between what had been and what would be, without thought or intention. Through all the challenges of her teens and the pride of her young-adult life, I remember that little girl covered in lipstick and mud as she retreated back, for just a bit longer, into her passing childhood.

It was some years later when I realized that summer, autumn, winter, and spring also have their liminal moments. These come as the seasons shift, something I now sense eight times a year instead of the usual four.

Equinoxes and solstices are noted on most calendars, and remarked upon by many:

"Where did the summer go?"

"Only ten more days till spring!"

On the spring and fall equinoxes, the rays of the Earth's daystar shine directly on the Equator where, for one moment, day and night will embrace as equals before the Earth continues her tilt.

As I write on this March morning, spring is two days old, though here in New England, we are in the midst of a cold rain that will turn to snow tonight. Seasons wax and wane like the moon, from tentative and new—trying out their warmth or chill before withdrawing like a shy child—to full and assured of their sear or bluster. They also have a point when they pivot, and sometimes, if we are very lucky, we take notice.

On another July morning several years after Megan graduated from high school and moved to New Orleans, I was lucky enough to notice. I had brewed my coffee and was stepping out onto the back stoop to plan my day in the garden, when I realize something was different, something had changed from the day before, though I wasn't sure what.

I walked around that day like a human question mark: What was it? What was I sensing? It took me all day, and then realization dawned as the sun set: summer had turned away from spring and toward autumn. The season was no longer in the business of growth and flowers, but in the setting and ripening of fruit and seed. We were at that point in the year when the days were still long, when dawn came early and the sun climbed high, shedding light evenly, but the plants and creatures were responding to something that was not readily evident to me in my twenty-first-century human comings and goings.

After that day, I began to pay more attention to the feel of the air, the tilt of the sun, and what was happening all around me. Did you know that as late summer approaches, the morning's birdsong reveille is replaced with an evening serenade of crickets looking for love? After a few days of heightened attention, I sat down to write about what I was learning and how I was learning it. This reflection comes from that time:

Janus has a twin; her name is July.
I met her on my back porch
just after sunrise on a summer morning.
I caught her in that miracle moment-between,
when she wore both faces with easy grace.
Facing east, she was the season passing,
though still in sight:

greening earth, and budding tree,
honey bees drunk on pollen and promise.
Facing west, she glowed with harvest,
pledged and set, though not yet realized.
In one moment, between my own greening,
and glowing, I saw.

That subtle "moment-between," glimpsed in both my daughter and the seasons, still captivates me. Since the summer day I first sensed the shift, I have found the same pivot point in the other three seasons. In early May, the spring finally responds to the wooing of the sun and commits fully to leaf and flower. Late October brings the release of summer's leaves, their color mimicking the glow of the sun that once made them unfurl themselves. And February's strengthening sun informs icicles and snow banks that their days are numbered.

Awareness is a quiet thing for me; I have received too many quizzical looks, followed by quick changes of conversation, to speak often of what I notice in the world. But sometimes, when I am (again) very lucky, I find someone with whom I can confide, and learn I am not alone.

In August of that year, a friend and I were enjoying a garden-fresh vegetarian lunch on a flowery patio when the subject turned to the weather. We both remarked on the long stretch of hot, sunny weather, before I ventured a comment about summer beginning to turn toward fall. My friend, Ann, smiled a small smile and nodded knowingly. I asked if she had sensed this too.

Oh, what a catastrophe for us when we cut ourselves off from the rhythm of the year, from our unison with the sun and the earth. Oh, what a catastrophe, what a maiming of love...cut off from the magic connection of the solstice and the equinox!

(D. H. LAWRENCE)

"Yes, these are the half seasons," she replied. "They're part of the pagan calendar." She then went on to inform me that for millennia, Earth-based traditions have not only sensed these subtle turnings but also celebrated them. I have had a good education in the Western traditions, but no one had ever told me about these half-seasons until Ann enlightened me.

As we finished our meal and sipped a ginger iced tea that made our taste buds sing, Ann told me about half-seasons and her experience of celebrating them. She spoke of bonfires and willow branches, candles and blessings. I was so intrigued by our conversation that I did further research.

Samhain (pronounced "sow-wen") falls on October 31, and in these traditions, is considered the first day of the new year and the start of winter. It is halfway between the autumnal equinox and winter solstice. When Christianity came along, Samhain became All Hallows' Eve. The people who clung to the old ways were called demon-worshippers, witches, and sorcerers, and the church taught that evil would be afoot that night in an effort to keep people from celebrating around bonfires. Frightened cottagers carved scary faces into turnips and gourds to keep the ghouls away, a tradition we continue with lit jack-o-lanterns on our doorsteps.

Imbolc is celebrated on February first, lambing time in the British Isles, where the celebration has ancient roots. An interesting aside: there is a tale of a divine crone named Cailleach who, on Imbolc, searches for enough firewood to see her through the remainder of winter. If winter is going to last a good while longer, she casts a spell to make the day bright and sunny so she can find enough wood. If spring is imminent, the day will be overcast. It seems that somehow, Cailleach has bequeathed her power to Punxsutawney Phil, and our imaginations are all the poorer for it.

Beltane, on May 1, is the celebration of the first day of summer. On May Day, people throughout villages and towns across Britain created garlands of greens and flowers to bedeck the May Pole (a fertility symbol). Young people danced around the pole to celebrate new life.

Lammas, at the end of July, a festival of the wheat harvest, was the half-season I noticed first; when summer "glowed with harvest, pledged and set, though not yet realized."

This wisdom I had discovered and held so close has been known and celebrated with ritual, fire, and food, since the dawn of human history. Because I was raised in a patriarchal tradition, a tradition that taught that Earth and Nature were less than desirable and, perhaps, downright dangerous for my soul, I knew these turning points as Halloween, Ground Hog's Day, and

May Day, little celebrations stripped of their history, mystery, and import. But now I know, and (as I have been known to tell others) once you know something, you cannot un-know it. Knowing changes us, and there is much to remember, notice, and learn if we humans are to reclaim a beneficent place in the web of life. The wisdom of the natural world is waiting to inform us; it has always been there, just under the surface of our stories of goblins and groundhogs.

In my sixtieth year, I am in a liminal space of my own, a "moment between my own greening and glowing," as are many of my friends and colleagues. No longer young and physically fertile, our life force is channeled into sustenance, wisdom, and legacy. Liminality acts as a lens, focusing the mind and spirit, so that what was once forgotten or obfuscated can be seen clearly. I find my attention has turned naturally to the influence my life will have had on the world and those I love. I spend less and experience more; create rather than produce, while kindness has become my life's goal. I am as strong and vital as a late-summer flower, deep and rich in hue, nourishing and flourishing, able to withstand gentle breezes or autumn gales and take it in stride. I have become strong, quiet, and confident in this mid-season of my life.

> *The sun shines different ways in winter and summer. We shine different ways in the seasons of our lives.*
>
> **(TERRI GUILLEMETS)**

Wisdom is pulling women and men out of our comfortable spaces and onto our own porches to notice that something is different. Everything is changing. Sitting in our rocking chairs or leaning against the railing, we, like Janus, can see what has passed and what is emerging. We can listen with all our senses to Nature's language, and we can choose to pay attention and celebrate all the turns and seasons of life. We can, again, know them as holy moments.

Reflection

The Latin word for threshold is *limina*, the space where you are not in one room or the other but in between both. Metaphorically, liminal spaces are encountered as we outgrow old beliefs and habits but have not yet fully entered into new ones. These are places of possibilities but places we cannot linger in for long.

- Take some time to learn more about your ancestors' ways of understanding the natural world. What wisdom can you glean for your own life?

- Can you name the liminal spaces of your own life? What space is currently yours?

- If "liminality acts as a lens, focusing the mind and spirit so that, what was once forgotten or obfuscated, can be seen clearly," what have your own liminal spaces brought to your attention? How have you changed after coming through those times and spaces?

Spirit,
You inhabit the thresholds,
the liminal spaces of my life.
Teach me to meet You here,
in these in-between places.
May I gather the strength of past seasons,
bringing it with me as I face
the next season of my life.

10

Cats and Birds

We are kindred all of us,
killer and victim,
predator and prey,
me and the sly coyote,
the soaring buzzard,
the elegant gopher snake
and trembling cottontail,
the foul worms
that feed on our entrails
all of them, all of us.

Long live diversity,
long live the earth!"

(EDWARD ABBEY)

*T*he polar vortex had descended into the temperate zone again, one of the unhappy effects of climate change, and the air was incredibly cold, even for February in Connecticut. As I opened the front door to retrieve that morning's *Hartford Courant*, hurrying against the cold, I barely noticed a little pile of fluff beside the welcome mat. I brought the paper in before my pre-caffeinated brain registered that the "fluff" was a tiny bird, a purple finch.

That its feathers were all fluffed out made sense; birds do this to create heat pockets near their bodies when they need to stay warm, and it was bone chilling outside. That it didn't fly away when I opened the door and retrieved the paper did not make sense. I pulled my heavy fleece bathrobe more tightly around my neck and stepped back into the visiting arctic. The "fluff" was still there, absolutely still.

For a moment I wondered if a neighborhood cat had left us a "gift" of its kill, but the bird's body did not appear to have undergone the trauma of an attack. I scooped it up and held it to my chest as I ducked back inside and shut the door. I walked into the kitchen, where the strengthening sun was just starting to come through the east window, and held the little bird up to see if it was still alive. It blinked its tiny black eyes at me but didn't move at all in any other way. I held it gently in one hand as I rummaged around the house for clean kitchen towels and an empty shoebox. I swaddled the little purple-red creature in a dishcloth and tucked it into the shoebox, which I placed on the table in a puddle of sun. I made the coffee, fed the dogs, and unloaded the dishwasher, before finally sitting down at the kitchen table to enjoy a cup of coffee and marvel at this tiny creature using my home as a warming station.

For two hours, all it did was sit in its dishcloth blanket and blink at me. When the finch finally began to flutter and shrug, I carried it back to the front door, unwrapped it and watched it fly away into the frigid blue sky. I wished it well.

Back then, I fed the birds all winter long, but not anymore. Now I feed the two remaining feral cats that were born in our woodpile several years ago. If I fed the birds, I would just be setting them up to become cat-supper. P.C. (pre-cats), though, I had positioned bird feeders so that they would be visible from my kitchen and dining room windows, and then purchased a little book titled *Birds of Connecticut*, which I kept on the kitchen table.

The feeders attracted finches, wrens, black-capped chickadees, and pairs of cardinals. We had mourning doves and woodpeckers, cowbirds, nuthatches, and starlings. My mother, who lived with my family at the time, loved to watch the birds come to the feeders. So did I. We would stand together at the windows and smile at their behaviors: chickadees came, took a seed, and then flitted off again to eat in peace while their sisters and brothers serenaded them: *chick-dee-dee-dee.* Blue jays chittered, cawed, and make a great mess by flinging the seed they didn't like onto the ground until they found the choice morsel they were looking for. Once they had their treasures, the jays flew to the branches of a high tree to eat. Mourning doves, beautiful, light gray creatures, feed only from the ground and verbalize, with a sound akin to the air running out of a set of bagpipes, when they are forced to take flight. Wrens and finches will feed from hanging feeders and the ground, wherever they can find a meal.

Birds are in trouble all around the globe. Their populations have plummeted as fields and forests have given way to a landscape of suburban lawns, factory farms, and paved roads, none of which provides sustenance for insects or birds. Birdseed, usually grown in great, mid-western, monoculture fields of millet and sunflower, is purchased in large bags from a big-box-store; it is not the perfect answer, but it is food for the hungry. Like any modern feedlot, however, metal and plastic feeders providing for large groups of animals can create health issues.

One early morning of the same year, when the frigid air had retreated to Canada and spring was almost in the air in Connecticut, I stepped outside to refill the feeders. Late winter and early spring are when wild birds are hungriest, any natural sources of fuel have long since been gobbled up, and the birds become reliant on human help to survive a situation we created for them with our quest for more land, bigger houses, and manicured landscapes.

A small group of wrens and finches were feeding on the bare driveway, and they all scattered as I dragged the heavy seed bucket across the pavement and lifted off the lid. As I scooped peanuts out of the container, I noticed that one tiny wren hopped a few feet away but did not take flight.

Now, I have secret aspirations of being like Francis of Assisi, who could commune with wild creatures, and for one moment, I hoped that (maybe, perhaps) the little bird sensed my spiritual kinship and kindness, and knew it didn't need to fear me. Then I looked closer.

The wren's eyes were swollen shut. I picked her up, and she sat stock-still in my gloved palm, blind, and probably terrified. I brought her into the house, found a safe container for her, and called the local Audubon Society office. The woman who answered the phone told me that there were many wild birds coming down with conjunctivitis that spring. Apparently, when they grab seeds from feeders, birds rub their beaks and eyes against the wire or plastic, and share germs with one another. This would not happen if there were still fields and meadows filled with last season's seeds to feast from, but humans giveth, and humans taketh away. Mostly we taketh away.

I threw my germ-ridden gloves in the washing machine and drove the little bird across the river to Glastonbury. For a "donation" of fifty dollars, the little wren would receive treatment for pink-eye, and be released into the wild once she was healed. I paid the "donation," and came home to swab the feeders with rubbing alcohol.

Two years later, and just as my home was becoming an established destination restaurant and medical center for avian species, our dogs began spending a lot of time sniffing around the edges of the woodpile stacked against the fence in the backyard. Because the dogs' noses know much more than I do about the other creatures with which I share my yard, I wondered what it was that interested the dogs so much. I began a "woodpile stakeout," watching and waiting for the suspected raccoon or woodchuck to make itself known. Instead, a skinny black cat jumped over the fence and disappeared into the spaces between the split logs. When I peeked between the chinks in the stacked wood, I heard the mewling of kittens and saw a pair of bright yellow eyes staring back at me.

The mama cat, who was barely more than a kitten herself, realized we knew where her babies were and promptly moved them from woodpile to a hollowed-out space beneath the tool shed. We pretended not to notice. In a few weeks, she began leading the pouncing, bouncing kits around the yard as she introduced them to the world.

Over the course of two years, the mama disappeared, along with several of her babies, while one of her surviving daughters became a mama with six kittens of her own. We had traded our weekly purchases of birdseed for cat chow, and knew we had to do something in the way of population control. My husband connected with a group of veterinarians in our state who help people care for feral kitties. They provided "Have a Heart" traps, with instructions to catch as many cats as possible by a set date, when the traveling surgery center would be in town. For the bargain price of $75 per cat, they would spay or neuter the animals, give them their rabies and leukemia shots, and return them that evening. We took up a collection from all the other neighborhood feral-cat enablers, caught the remaining mother and her five adolescents, and the procedures were performed.

In the last three years, five cats have lost their lives to cars, weather, and infection. The remaining two are sleek, fat, and healthy. They have lost most of their fear of my family and allow themselves to be petted and scratched. On a warm day, you can often find them rolling, stretching, and napping on my sunny front walk. Despite their full bellies, they still hunt rodents and birds, like their step-brother, Jerry.

Jerry is our only house cat, or more honestly, our daughter Elizabeth's semi-house cat. He came to live with us when Elizabeth moved home after a breakup, and he stayed through one more going and coming. She named him Jerry after her favorite musician, Jerry Garcia, of the Grateful Dead.

Like his namesake, Jerry has never been a creature to follow the rules of polite society. He began as an indoor kitty, as is politically correct in these days of helicopter pet-parents. He didn't stay that way. Within two summer weeks of his residence, he had pushed every screen out of every open window in an absolute refusal to sit on a sill and watch the world go by. We repaired the window screens and surrendered to his will.

Jerry, now about seven years old, is a tomcat in every way except for his ability to "tom." He is huge. He sleeps all day, stays out all night, and is the stuff of nightmares for every little chipmunk or bird that might take a liking to our English-garden-style yard in central Connecticut.

One morning last summer, I woke to the sound of terror coming through my bedroom window, a desperate chirping and chittering that all parents, whether they cheep, moo, or speak, register in their gut as a cry for help. I grabbed my eyeglasses from the bedside table and scampered around the bed to the window. The sky was just turning pink with the rising August sun, and in the diffuse light, I saw him: a thick-middled, slinking, gray-striped cat, with a bird in his mouth. The bird was a fledging meadowlark whose parents had nested in the blue spruce and were now going berserk from the spreading branches of the chestnut tree.

Nature is dark and light, birth and death. Everything and its opposite. And in nature there are predators and prey. The hunters and the hunted. The heartbreakers and the heartbroken.

(LYNN WEINGARTEN)

I grabbed my robe from the end of the bed and ran down the stairs, hearing my husband's words "leave it alone" fade behind me. I flew out the back door, down the steps, and onto the dew-soaked grass. Jerry was nowhere in sight, so I sprinted in the direction of his favorite hiding place, under the hydrangeas that line the back of the house. Momma and Papa Meadowlark were still raising a racket, swooping in panic from chestnut tree to clothesline to lawn.

In August, the hydrangeas are heavy with blue-balled blossoms, and my rustling in them must have startled Jerry into loosening his grip on the young bird. The chick came out from under the bushes racing like a road-runner. I tossed my robe over him to calm him and keep him safe, while I grabbed Jerry by the nape of his neck and hauled him up into my arms. I scolded him in unison with Mr. Meadowlark as I ascended the back-steps and pushed him into the kitchen.

Daddy bird was now on the clothesline just above my head, still giving the world a piece of his mind. Mommy bird watched and called from the relative safety of the high-backed bench beneath the chestnut tree.

I walked back to my robe lying lightly on the ground and, very carefully, lifted it, inch by inch, until baby bird was free. He resumed his open-winged, road-runner impersonation until physics and fear lifted him off the ground and he flew, now in formation between his parents, to the leafy safety of the blackberry bushes.

Jerry still hunts and haunts the creatures in our backyard. And the meadowlarks have returned this spring to take their chances and nest again in the concealing branches of the spiky blue spruce. Nature may be merciless, but she is endlessly hopeful.

Reflection

I really do have aspirations of being like Saint Francis, and have always loved the creatures around me. What about you?

- What is your relationship with the other animals with which we share the planet?
- How do you make space for them? How does your life impact theirs?
- How does your spiritual life inform your choices and actions when it comes to the rest of creation?
- Can you think of ways you have noticed both the mercilessness and the hopefulness of Nature? How do both qualities relate to human life? Do you think more is expected of humans—and if so, why?

Teach me, Spirit,
to care for Your creation.
Teach me
to live in harmony with You.

11

Waiting

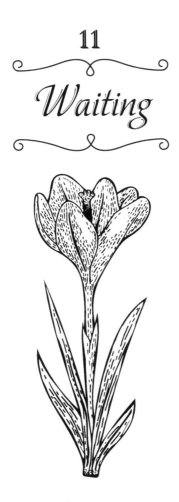

The greatest prayer is patience.

(THE BUDDHA)

*T*oday is a waiting day. I am waiting for inspiration. I am waiting for the pie to come out of the oven. I am waiting to close my eyes for an hour after a night spent coughing instead of sleeping. I am waiting for this upper respiratory infection to go away. I am watching the north wind whip the tops of the pine trees and the American flag across the street while I wait for the next warm day. I am waiting for spring, waiting to finish my thesis, waiting for the grief of three losses in six winter weeks to abate.

Much of my time in the garden is spent waiting, though not usually as impatiently as I wait in early spring. Vernal waiting is hardest of all because I've been waiting all winter.

A tiny purple crocus is blooming outside my back door. Just one. Today is April first and I wonder whether winter is pranking me on this April Fool's Day. The meteorologists are saying that there is a good chance we may get hit with a Nor'easter two days from now; the first one of this winter, now that it is spring. We just have to wait and see what develops. I remember another early April when a late-season snowstorm deposited about a foot of snow overnight before ushering in a warm front. It is the only time I can ever recall my children wearing short sleeves and gloves as they created slush men all across the backyard.

I am worried about my rhubarb plants; they seemed less robust last summer, and I am wondering whether they are past their prime. I am planning to fertilize them deeply with horse manure from my brother's little two-horse farm to see if I can strengthen them. Only time will tell, and it won't tell me anything yet. I am waiting for that horse manure to be delivered, and for the next warm, dry day to apply it before covering it with compost that needs to be dug out of the three bins that are ready. Digging the compost has to wait for calm winds, dry paths, and the manure. That is how it works. Waiting to do more waiting.

The apple, pear, and cherry trees appear quiescent, buds still tightly closed, not even a hint of green leaves. I know that at this time of year, though I cannot see it, trees are coursing with life, pulling sugary sap up from their roots and moving it from trunk to branches as the sun strengthens and the nights move from freezing to temperate. The pears, a Bosc and a Bartlett, are old gals, well-established and good producers. I wonder whether they will be inundated with pear-midges like two years ago, or not bothered by them at all, like last year. It is all in the timing, and the timing is influenced by the weather. Bloom early or late, and the midges lose their window of opportunity to deposit fertilized eggs into the newborn pears. Bloom in concert with midge-mating, and provide a flowery pink and white nursery. It is up to the trees and the temperatures. All I can do is see what happens.

The three apples and one self-pollinating cherry are babies, little more than saplings this year. I wonder whether they survived the winter, whether they will flower, or only leaf-out. I must bide my time until they show me. In the meantime, I peel grass back from their trunks and add bio-char and compost to the exposed soil. Soon, I will get some wood chips and cover the soil four inches deep.

The sequoia died over the winter. My son brought it home from a trip to the Boston Science Museum about ten years ago, a twig in a clear plastic tube. I planted it not knowing whether it would survive the crazy swings of Connecticut's climate. It lived and grew for ten years, and then it died. We had a warm day on Saturday, so my husband took it down and dragged it to the side of the road, where the town workers will pick it up and make mulch of it. Sequoias like the world to be wet and temperate. Connecticut weather makes no promises.

The American chestnut tree that I planted at about the same time as the Sequoia is huge, twenty-feet tall, with a canopy to match. American chestnut trees are rare after a blight infected them at the turn of the twentieth century. Scientists estimate that between three and four billion trees died in forty years. So far, my tree is thriving and shows no evidence of the yellow cankers that would forecast its doom. It has produced tender nuts in round, prickly shells for the last three years. We shall see if it continues to beat the odds.

Adopt the pace of nature; her secret is patience.

(RALPH WALDO EMERSON)

I bought the tree from an older Italian man who had fruit trees for sale from his driveway. He lived in a nondescript raised ranch in the dip of a hilly road in Wethersfield, Connecticut. I also bought a lemon tree and a fig tree, and tucked all three trees into the back of my Prius. The man told me about his fruit trees and invited me into his "backa-yard" to see them. He had apples, plums, cherries, and peaches, and a beautiful vegetable garden about twice the size of mine.

I asked him how he did it. He pointed to a long, low building behind us. "Chickens. You gotta hava da chickens!" He sent me home with a head of butter lettuce as big as a cabbage and as sweet and tender as new life.

I am waiting to get chickens; waiting until I am not always so busy, waiting until I don't have a summer trip planned, until I can afford the coop, yard, and other equipment. Maybe I will sell eggs. More likely I will give them away to family and friends. The poop is what is most valuable anyway, the stuff of life. I will compost it and wait for it to leach its ammonia and lose its stink before spreading it around my butter lettuce, blueberries, and brussels sprouts.

Waiting isn't always about outcomes. Sometimes it is done purely for its own sake; in anticipation of nothing in particular. This is the best waiting to do.

On warm days, I like to sit in the sweet straw of the garden as the day ends. In late afternoon, the sun no longer blazes and burns the skin. Its light and warmth are more like a lover's slow caress; it arouses a deepening and catching of breath as tired muscles become soft and languid.

Relaxed, I can see the world full of life all around me: tiny grass spiders hunting

At some point in life, the world's beauty becomes enough.

(TONI MORRISON)

houseflies for their supper, bees covered in yellow dust flying from borage to calendula to sunflower, green and yellow striped swallowtail caterpillars munching on fennel and dill. If I move the straw away from the soil, I see worm castings that resemble tiny lunar craters pocking the dark, moist dirt.

If the neighbors aren't cutting their grass or playing loud music as they wash their cars, I can hear birdsong, bee buzz, and the wind ruffling the blackberry leaves as I wait for nothing and find I am a part of everything.

Reflection

In our busy society, where "time is money," waiting is to be avoided. Before the Industrial Revolution, though, when most of us still sang in unison with the land we tended and depended upon, waiting was as important as action. Plant too soon, and you might lose your crop to frost. Harvest too soon, and your grain and fruit would be unfit for consumption. Human beings learned to wait, and to fill their waiting with meaning. Christmas and Easter, the highest holidays of the Christian calendar, were preceded by times of waiting and preparation.

- How do you wait? Are you patient or impatient?
- What are you willing to wait for?
- How has busyness affected your life? What has it added? What has it taken from you?

Teach me, Spirit,
to wait patiently,
content in each moment,
for You are always present.

12

Brother Love

Siblings are branches of a tree...
they fruit, they grow,
till they die and fall.

(OMANI SHED)

"*I* miss that kid." My brother spoke the words into
the warm air of the backyard, his head turned

slightly away. I could hear tears in the tremble of his voice.

"I never thought this would happen. I *knew* he would beat the cancer. I had no idea that this evil fungus would kill him. I thought he would walk out of that hospital." He paused, swallowed, took a few breaths. "It never crossed my mind." He turned toward me. "But you know, even if I knew I would only get eighteen years with him, I would do it all again."

I smiled a tiny encouraging smile, and he continued. "I would spend more time with him, though. I spent a lot of time with him, but I would spend more."

"You are a good dad, Michael."

"I know. I love my kids. I love my grandchildren."

I let the silence sit with us. We had gotten used to it, after having barely spoken for years before our mother was diagnosed with cancer, the same disease that his son had battled. We lived different lives, as we had always done. It was life events that brought us back together again for however long, as they had always done.

I looked more closely at my younger sibling, noting the new lines in his face, as he told me that he had picked up the phone to call his youngest son just two days earlier, and then had remembered. Remembering is risky business.

I asked about his wife. "She has good days and bad days. Mostly bad days. But we help each other. We are on the same page." I told him I was glad. It was the truth.

"I still haven't prayed. I am too angry."

"Anger can be a prayer," I told him.

He tilted his head upward. "Where the fuck were you? I wanted to hear from you. I wanted to know you were there. I miss my son." He ended with a sob and wiped his eyes on the back of his hand before glancing sideways at me.

I nodded. "That was prayer."

He nodded back, then stretched his legs out and stood up from where we were sitting on the back steps, eating frittata off plates balanced on our knees. He had gained weight in the seven weeks since his child had been buried.

"You're going to have a good garden this year," he predicted.

"Yes," I agreed. "Thank you again for the horse manure."

"I'll bring you some more," he said. "It will be a good reason for a visit. I miss you."

"I'll take a visit, however you fit it in. I miss you, too."

We walked down to the garden so I could dig up and pot the five blackberry canes he wanted. He also took the little ornamental cherry I had potted up last summer, hoping to find someone who would give it a good home. I showed him the three young apple trees, the tiny fruiting cherry, its buds just starting to swell in the April sunshine, and the two elders whose berries would be ready for harvest later in the year. We walked under the skeletal grapevines on their arbor; they wouldn't leaf-out for another month at least.

"Look at the size of that vine!"

"Daddy planted those the first year I lived here." I told him.

He nodded. We share a history that needs little narrative.

We walked back up the length of the yard, and then we loaded plants and empty manure barrels into his truck. We hugged. Then, while he drove back to East Lyme and the boat he was preparing for the water, I began spreading horse poop around the fruiting plants.

As I worked, my memories spooled out. When my brother was little and wanted a story, we would lie in his twin bed under the blue cotton bedspread. He would curl up close, and we would cry together as I read about the little bird that fell from its nest. Its words—"Are you my mother?"—always tugged at our hearts.

Before an operation at age eight, my brother's ears stuck straight out on either side of his blonde head, little pale wings that became translucent when the sun was low behind him. I held his hand to comfort him, as I confronted, with words bigger than both of us, the taunting, laughing, older boys. He clung to me and hid behind me, and I protected him from everyone but myself.

We competed for our mother's approval. I told him he was stupid. He told me I was fat and ugly. He hated school, because he believed me that he was stupid. I was quite heavy, and believed him that I was fat and ugly.

Mostly, though, we loved each other. Together we built forts in the woods, went on bike-hikes, splashed in the brook, played baseball and kickball in the street, fought with and for each other, and made "secret recipes" by mixing my father's shaving soap with lotion and perfume in the bathroom sink, shrieking and laughing at the smelly goop that formed as my mother tried to ignore our noise.

Things were different as we grew, and our social circles expanded. He chafed under the rules my parents set, and he moved out. My mother worried, especially when my brother got sick living in an unheated trailer in January. The police chief came to our house one Saturday afternoon and told my father that Michael was really ill and needed to come home. My father went to get him.

"My house, my rules," my father said, and Michael was so sick he agreed. He was seventeen. My parents were frightened for him. I was furious. We ignored one another.

He found a job in the kitchen of a restaurant, and then found he had a gift and passion for cooking. He came to play with my kids, "wrassling" with them and holding them in huge, tight bear-hugs. He was like my dad in that. He was fun and physical, and he loved them to bits. We laughed and shared meals.

He became a chef. He married and started a family. They were busy, we were busy. The kids, my three and his four, brought us together regularly for birthday parties and the occasional holiday celebration. The kids grew up, first mine, then his. We got together less often. We lived different lives.

Years passed. I received an occasional call when he wanted to talk. I called him when there was something to say. The advent of text messaging helped. Typical messages went like this: "At the ER with Mom. Will keep you posted." Information without emotion. We both held onto the information because it was what we had.

Last June, I got a call. "Austyn has a tumor in his lungs. Laura is bringing him to Yale." We began to talk in weekly updates.

Last November, I called him. "Mom has cancer. They don't know if she will get through Christmas." For two months, he came to the house to visit my mother as often as he could. He slept wherever his son was, Smilow Cancer Center or home, and worked days. It was a lot for him. He made it a point to come with me to make initial arrangements at the funeral home. "I want to be involved."

Our brothers and sisters are there with us from the dawn of our personal stories to the inevitable dusk.

(SUSAN SCARF MERRELL)

By the time my mother died in the first days of January, his son was going through the final and most intense round of chemotherapy. Michael was exhausted. After our mother's memorial service on January 11, I didn't see my brother again until I hugged him four weeks later in the receiving line at his son's funeral service.

Back in my own yard, I realized that today had been the first time I had seen him since then, seven weeks ago. He calls me a few times a week when he is low, or just to check in. I send quick messages: "How are you doing, brother?" He is busy, I am busy. Days and weeks go by.

Someday, one of us will pass from this life, and the other will be left alone with the hurts, hopes, and memories that siblings carry. Those memories are both scars and beacons.

Reflection

I love my brother. Like most familial love, our love is fraught by tensions from the past, and the stresses of the present. Love is a complicated thing. It is simple, elemental, but it is not easy, especially when we have expectations (and we all have expectations).

If you have siblings, spend some contemplative time remembering the stories of your family. What are some of the hurts, hopes and memories you carry as "scars and beacons"? How do those things affect your relationship? What do you want or need to apologize for? What would you heal if possible?

Spirit of Love,
I am grateful for siblings,
both those of blood and those of the heart.
May I give to them,
even as I receive from them.

13

Blight and Ivy

Imagine to yourselves a being like Nature,
boundlessly extravagant, boundlessly indifferent...
how could you live in accordance
with such indifference?

(FRIEDRICH NIETZSCHE)

*G*ardens are a human attempt to contain and plan Nature. Nature sometimes humors us for a time but never for very long. For every promise of spring, there are summer disappointments, and the reckoning of autumn when mistakes and the scars of the land are laid bare. I have become the keeper of a particular bit of the planet; I live and work in and on it, and it lives and works in and on me.

My garden's soil was thin and lifeless when I first tilled the space and began to amend it. Over the last quarter century, I have piled leaves, grass clippings, straw, and compost over the rocky ground; it is making a difference, but only incrementally, one-eighth inch at a time. I no longer till, not wanting to disturb the life in the soil. This year, I have spread horse manure as a "side-dressing" along all the garden's planned rows. I also have a driveway full of wood chips to trundle down and lay over the soil and poop. We shall see if, and how, they grow the life of the soil and benefit the garden.

Alternaria solani is my bitter enemy and most persistent disappointment. It is a soil-born fungus commonly known as early blight. It prefers (and can kill) plants in the nightshade family: tomatoes, peppers, and eggplant; unfortunately, because I would prefer those plants live and produce, the battle lines are drawn. Every summer, the fungus and I wage war; some years it gains ground and some years I beat it back, but the war never ends, and it has its own version of collateral damage.

One year, several years back, my vegetable garden was getting away from me (as it always does).

I needed help. I decided to invite several friends to use it as a communal-garden. We didn't all have our own plots (as in the community-garden model); instead we purchased seeds and seedlings, planted them, tended them, and harvested them all together. We started the season with lots of enthusiasm and a shared meal. I ordered a load of composted manure, and together we trundled it in wheelbarrows from the front driveway down to the vegetable garden. We purchased seed potatoes; packages of seeds for lettuce, chard, kale and collards; and flats of tomatoes, eggplant and peppers seedlings (everyone's favorite summer produce).

June was a beautiful month that summer: warm and mostly dry, with no weather surprises. Everything in the garden came up, established healthy roots, and our mouths watered in anticipation of juicy tomatoes with just a touch of salt and olive oil.

July came. A very wet and windy July. By happenstance, that wet and windy July occurred in the same year that one of the "big box stores" ordered all its tomato seedlings from the same Florida grower. That grower didn't know it, but their seedlings were infected with early blight. People bought those seedlings in good faith and planted them. When the bad weather set in, the blight spores exploded from the soil and were carried by the wind from one neighborhood garden to the next. By the third week in July, all the tomatoes in our garden were infected, though we had purchased them from a local grower.

We say that Nature is cruel, but what we really mean is that Nature refuses to behave herself according to our priorities.

(STUART LOCKE)

We made special compost teas to strengthen the plants: warm water mixed with cow manure and garden compost. We watered ever so carefully, being sure that the tea did not splash onto the leaves and increase the spread of the fungus. Every morning, we pulled dozens of yellowing, blighted leaves off the plants while praying that the weather would break, and the vines would produce fruit from new and healthy growth. The weather did not break, and the blight spread. It killed all the tomatoes before going after the chilis and aubergines. I pulled the plants out of the ground and burned them. The smoke rose from the fire pit like a dispiriting incense, taking the group's joy with it. My friends stopped coming, even though the pears produced a bumper crop, and we had enough kale, collards, and chard to feed an army.

I invite friends every year, and they come once, maybe twice, and then the summer takes them away. War is not for the faint-hearted or half-committed. Neither is gardening.

I soldier on, mulching deeply, companion planting, pinching back, and leaving lots of space between plants so that the air can move and flow between them. Tomatoes are annual vines, but the blight is perennial, rising like a summer-vampire, looking for new victims, being little deterred by garlic, compost, or my curses.

While blight attacks from the soil of the garden, poison ivy invades from my northern flank, crossing my neighbor's yard and climbing his rusting fence before sending itchy tendrils across the lawn to slither up my young dogwood and surround the baby elder in a living, rash-producing-cage.

My husband and children are all highly allergic to poison ivy; I am much less so. At regular intervals from March through November, I don long pants and sleeves along with leather elbow gloves. I gather my clippers and a lawn-waste bag and trek around the yard pulling the clingy vines up and out, to cut them and tuck them carefully into the heavy black plastic. I am not getting ahead of this particular invader, just keeping it enough at bay to enjoy the yard and protect my loved ones from red bumps and days of suffering. The war will only be won when an arborist takes down my neighbor's dying pines, and pulls up the mother ivy by her roots.

Until then, the vines twirl and swirl across our property lines. Like blight spores, like all of Nature, they are no respecter of human boundaries. Those imaginary lines we draw between properties (and between nations) exist only in our minds. Nature knows better.

Reflection

I am very aware that my garden is planted in the soil of the world, a world where poison ivy and blight existed long before human beings cultivated tomatoes or apple trees.

It helps me to remember that Nature includes no sense of "mine." Neither does it classify tomatoes as good and blight as bad. Those are judgements I make.

Keeping this in mind, consider the things about our natural world (especially those you interact with in your own ecosystem) that frighten, frustrate, or anger you. How do you deal with them? How do they deal with you? How might you make peace with the unknown?

You know, Spirit,
how I hate to surrender my control;
how much I want to say, "Mine!"
Teach me to make peace
with what I can't control.
Remind me to make room in my life
for the uncontrollable, the unknowable,
for You.

14

Trees

For in the true nature of things,
if we rightly consider,
every green tree is far more glorious
than if it were made of gold and silver.

(MARTIN LUTHER)

The pear tree was so big that my father needed a fruit picker on a long pole to harvest from the middle branches. He stood beneath the tree with my grandfather and our neighbors Gino and Sammy Mancata, as he balanced and reached with the top-heavy tool and brought the sweet, ripe pears down from their branches.

These pears were divided equally between the bushel baskets lined up near the edge of the garage. All the neighborhood mothers were waiting for those bushels of pears: canning jars sterilized, peeling knives at the ready. My father did not want me underfoot, so he made me sit on the cement back steps to watch as the men, in long, dark cotton pants and white undershirts, cigarettes hanging from their lips, harvested the pears.

The *Prunus domestica* (Italian plum) grew over my sandbox behind the detached garage. It shaded me from the summer sun as I created castles and moats with my rusty pail and shovel. The tree's bark was smooth and dark, its low-flung branches filled with oblong purple plums with sweet, yellow flesh. Some of those plums were so swollen with juice that, on hot days, they would pop their skin. Sugars would ooze out of the rips and thicken to a syrup along the crease that always formed from the stem to blossom end. These are my earliest memories of trees; I was three or four years old.

I have a thing for trees; they are woven into all the memories of my life. I plant them, tend them, and sit in their shade. I have been known to hug them. I cry for them. I listen to them as they speak their strange, murmuring language of sighs and rustles, creaks, scents, and colors. I have leaned on their strength. My arboretum (also known as my yard) has chestnut, apple, pear, linden, birch, Japanese maple, elder, cherry, dogwood, spruce, and oak trees. The oak trees are gifts from the squirrels who stored acorns and forgot where they were. Unfortunately, the squirrels hid their acorns in my vegetable patch, so I have dug the oak seedlings up and potted them, until I find them good homes. Their parent was taken down in its prime by a neighbor. I cried from my living room window as I watched life and beauty fall, without reason, to a power saw and wood chipper.

I spent my formative years living on a corner lot across one street from a wooded swamp and brook, and the other from a hayfield ringed with old trees, while, on the next block, there was an undeveloped lot we called "the woods." All the neighborhood children gathered in the woods, where we had worn pathways to its corners and center with our feet and bicycle tires. Entering from the Fowler Avenue path, you could fork right to my favorite spot, a little dirt clearing where the canopy allowed sunlight to warm us. We regularly built forts in whatever corner we liked best: mini-homesteads complete with designated living space and whatever else our childhood imaginations deemed necessary.

The hayfield was owned by Mrs. Neiman, and she was kind enough to let us sled down its big hill in winter and play in the tall grasses closest to our homes during the summer. To get to the field, we needed to cross through a narrow band of trees. I had a favorite tree there, a tree that grew in the space between home and play, the largest tree in that woodland belt.

A child tripping down the steep dirt path would view the tree set against the straw hues of the grasses behind it. It was an old, old, apple tree, wild and wide, nothing like the pruned and puny trees of the local orchards. The tree held out one branch the way a grandmother holds out her arms to gather you in; the branch grew long and low, parallel to the ground beneath it. It was just wide enough to accommodate our bottoms when we climbed to sit amid the pink blossoms, green leaves, and hard, small, wormy apples that grew wherever a twig had reached out from the rough bark to find the sun.

Between every two pine trees there is a door leading to a new way of life.

(JOHN MUIR)

We dubbed the space the "Monkey's Playhouse" (thinking ourselves akin to a band a macaques as we climbed and swung and jumped), and often met there to plan our days. If you were first to arrive, you could claim the hollow where the branch joined the trunk and made a saddle. It was the best spot on the tree. If you were alone, you could sit quietly where the breeze would find you among all the other wild creatures as they buzzed, trilled, and courted, and you could remember your own child-spirit and how you belonged to the whole, wide Earth.

The trees around the brook were willows that hung their trailing branches low, low, into the stream as it moved slowly toward the Connecticut River and, from there, into Long Island Sound. Swamp maples ringed the low spots around the wetlands, giving us handholds as we squished through the soft, soggy earth to stomp on an emerging skunk cabbage before we ran away laughing at the stench.

Our postage-stamp yard contained a mature, white dogwood that, like the Monkey's Playhouse, welcomed little climbers up into its branches. Every spring, the tree would burst into bloom long before her leaves unfurled. Dogwood blossoms have four petals, each tipped with a rusty stain. The knobby stamens (at the center) are a tan color. Being a spiritual child, I remember my father's cousin, Connie Carta, telling me the Sicilian folk story that the cross of Christ had been made from a dogwood tree, and the tree had been so ashamed to be used as an instrument of torture for the gentle man who taught us to love, that from that day forward, its wood became too soft to ever build with again, and every Easter, it bore flowers in the shape of a bloodied cross with the crown of thorns at the center.

I said to the almond tree, "Friend, speak to me of God," and the almond tree blossomed.

(NIKOS KAZANTZAKIS)

One year, when I was nine or ten, the dogwood came under attack from an invasion of gypsy moth caterpillars. My father pulled their web-like "tents" off as many branches as he could, dousing them in lighter fluid and setting them afire. He also wrapped the tree's trunk in two sided tape to trap the many-legged invaders, but there were so many that the dead created a bridge for the living, and the leaves still became caterpillar fodder. To save my beloved tree, I set myself the gory and disgusting task of squishing and scraping the wrigglers from the joints where the branches met the tree's trunk. Caterpillars bleed green, and their soft, little bodies curl in shock as you pierce their skin and smear their guts across the rough, gray bark. It made me retch, but I was filled with righteous anger against the squirmy creatures, and I grimly set about their annihilation armed with a stick and a vengeance.

When my family moved to the old farmhouse in Cromwell the year I was fourteen, we had one mature tree, a sugar maple. The tree grew just across from the driveway and shaded the picnic table, Weber Grill, and lawn chairs. In the fall, its leaves turned deep, deep, red before falling in drifts that my father raked and spread across the soil of his vegetable garden.

At the top of our property, along its western edge, was a small woodlot. My friends and I would go sit in those woods to cough and hack as we tried smoking cigarettes and marijuana, planning reconnaissance missions when the neighbor's plum trees were filled with ripe fruit, and we were high and hungry. The woods provided cover as we scoped the situation and dashed into the open, to grab two or three red plums before diving back into the undergrowth to giggle and gorge as we flouted the laws of property and possession.

When my husband and I bought our first (and only) home in central Connecticut, its front and backyards were dominated by Norway maple trees. Norway maples are considered invasive, but we did not know that then, and for years we enjoyed their shade and foliage without a tinge of environmental guilt. In the thirty-odd years we have lived here, we have lost all those maples to old age and weather. The trees on my property now are all youngsters, and I chose them with an eye to ecological diversity.

In the center of my front yard is a linden tree with its beautiful teardrop shape and incredibly sweet perfume when in flower. The tree is about twenty feet tall now, surrounded by a mulched circle where narcissus bob and dance in the winds of spring. I was widening that circle two days ago (heavy work, indeed) when I found a tiny American toad that had been hibernating beneath the sod. This little creature was a baby, about half the size of my thumb, and I had disturbed its slumber with my digging. Thankfully, it was unharmed. I found an old clay pot and a stone and made a shelter, a toad house, by turning the pot upside down and elevating one end by resting it on the stone. As I continued to work around the tree, I spied it trying out its new digs by hopping out and back in several times. Later in the day, a robin sat in the linden's bare branches above all the fresh-turned soil and chirped and trilled, claiming its newfound worm-hunting grounds. I hoped it wouldn't eat my little friend.

Toads are rare in suburban yards now. We Americans mow and cut and poison most everything—and amphibians, with their breathable skin, are very sensitive to their environments.

When I was in elementary school, our four-times-daily walk (we had to go home for lunch, then back for the afternoon) took us past a farm pond. Every year, there would come a warm day in May when our normal way home became impassable. Thousands of tiny, grey toads would be leaving the pond, hopping on and over one another, across sidewalks and roads to find new solitary homes under rocks and bushes, in gardens and cellar hatchways, where they could live their quiet lives swallowing mosquitos and beetles. We children would sit and watch this river of life flow right before our eyes, before turning and taking the back roads home.

My backyard is where the fruit and nut trees live, all pruned and planted to capitalize on sunshine and fruit production. They are joined by a "volunteer" white dogwood that has grown around the wire fence that separates my backyard from my neighbor's yard. The fence disappears into the tree's trunk, and reemerges on the other side. I like it that trees take property lines so lightly.

The only other "nonproductive" trees behind the house are a beautiful blue spruce, a small black birch, and a fragile ornamental cherry. The spruce was a "freebie," a little, blue-needled stick in a cardboard tube, given out to anyone who wanted one at a local state fair. The cherry was a Mother's Day gift from my son and his wife. The spruce is about twelve feet tall now and half as wide. Its branches sweep the grass and shelter nesting birds safely within its prickly arms. The birch, like its dogwood cousin, straddles a fence. The cherry bursts into pink flowers each April, like a colorful dinner bell for hungry bees.

Trees are matter made into memory. Their rings carry the history of their lives in narrow and wide bands of growth, feast and famine mapped into their interior lives, records we are not privy to until the tree falls or is felled. They live lives on a different scale than our own.

On a trip to Devon, England, I came across a strand of ancient, sweet chestnut trees growing in the gardens of Dartington Hall. Dartington traces its history back to the Norman Conquest of England in 1066. The hall was built in the twelfth century by a half-brother of King Richard II, and later, was part of the wedding gift Henry VIII gave to his sixth wife, Katherine Parr. Today, it is known for its beautiful gardens and history. The sweet chestnuts, planted in a row five hundred years ago, are part of the gardens on the ridge overlooking the (still intact) tilting field.

As I walked toward those trees, I was aware of their size and age, and my own. The tree trunks twisted and writhed, peeled and merged, to support the immense canopy and the flocks of noisy magpies that nested to raise their chicks in the immense branches. I felt called to the hollowed, hallowed places inside the living trees, places large enough for a human being to stand and sit, and I accepted the trees' invitation to be with them.

I chose a tree toward the center of the stand, where fewer human sounds would reach me, and stepped inside. Immediately, I was surrounded by a cool, dry, stillness. I felt the weight of branches above me, though I had no part in supporting that weight. I sat on the dry earth where once a tree's heartwood had formed, and then died and crumbled to sawdust. I rested my shoulders against the back of this living cavern and let myself relax into a life other than my own.

I don't know how long I sat there, only that time's passage was measured by light and shadow rather than numbers on a clock. The tree paid no more mind to me than it would have paid to a squirrel or spider seeking shelter in it. I knew that all around me, and without a thought about the middle-aged woman sitting at its center, the tree was drawing nutrients up from the remains of the primeval forest that had covered the land long before people cut down the trees and planted crops, while high above me, its leaves collected sunlight and turned it into food—a miracle if ever there was one.

Trees are sanctuaries. Whoever knows how to speak to them, whoever knows how to listen to them, can learn the truth.

(HERMANN HESSE)

The next day I visited the ancient yew that grew in the chapel's graveyard. Scientists believe the tree sprouted circa 500 CE, making it about 1500 years old. Its burled trunk is squat and heavy, rooted ponderously into the soil west of the tower (the only part of the church that remains after the same Henry dissolved the monasteries and Catholic churches). The tree's roots must spread for yards and yards into the soil, around the bones and buttons of the people laid to rest in Saint Mary's churchyard. I imagine some of what they were, carbon and iron, calcium and magnesium, are now a part of the ancient tree with its great, drooping branches.

Toward the end of my stay, I joined with others in a "Walk Through Deep Time," with Schumacher College's Dr. Stephan Harding. Dr. Harding is one of the thought-leaders in Gaia Theory—seeing the planet as a living system. According to Gaia Theory, there is a consciousness in all of creation, a wisdom that we are part of, but not able to translate with human intellect alone.

Our first step on the walk represented the Big Bang. Our final step brought us to the present. In between, we walked 4.6 kilometers (representing 4.6 billion years), taking us from the birth of the sun to the emergence of *Homo sapiens*. Our walk took us through the old growth forests along the River Dart in Devon, a place where mystery and myth are in the air, and the forest spirits survive (if one has the senses to find them).

Dr. Harding has honed his senses. Before we were ten steps into the understory, he stopped the group and asked us to find "the guardian of the forest." We looked around us. We peered at the ground. We creased our foreheads in puzzlement. Then one of the participants looked up and saw it: an old tree growing on the edge of the forest had split halfway up its height and fallen back upon itself in the shape of a stag's head and chest. Moss and leaves dripped from the "antlers" and "shoulders," as the stag hung its head over the path, regarding every creature that walked it, including us. The guardian must have approved our presence, because there were no mishaps along the way despite the muddy paths and the downpour that soaked our picnic lunches.

No ancient trees or old growth forests are left in Connecticut; the colonizing settlers took care of that in short order. The oldest tree in Connecticut, the Pinochet Sycamore planted near the Farmington River in Simsbury, is thought to be between two and three hundred years old. Still, individual trees carry the DNA of their predecessors, DNA set down during the Carboniferous Period (300 to 360 million years ago.)

Scientists are finally starting to understand the consciousness of trees. They communicate with one another through mycorrhizal networks, root systems sensing when another tree in their community is struggling or under attack from insects. They shunt nutrients from one to another and send out distress signals that allow other trees to prepare for threats from other creatures. I imagine they must have quite an alarm when it comes to human beings.

Our local trees have taken a beating in recent years, due mostly to climate change and lack of human understanding and planning. Almost a decade ago now, I remember Bob Maxon, a meteorologist on Connecticut's NBC channel, saying, "Some computer models are predicting a major snow storm next week." That particular model was an outlier, and no one really believed it; it was only the third week of October. Many trees were still in full leaf.

When the snow began to fall after nine o'clock on the night of October 29, 2011, it came down in fat, heavy flakes, sticking to everything. We heard the first cracks and thumps of branches and trunks collapsing around ten that night. The power was out before midnight, and it did not come back on until the afternoon of November 5. Most towns in the state cancelled trick-or-treating that year; there were too many downed trees and power lines for anyone to be safe. We lost our last big maple tree in that storm.

All winter long, the Connecticut landscape looked like the Ardennes Forest after the Battle of the Bulge: trees looked like matchsticks, splintered and ruined. It wasn't until the next May that new growth covered the scars.

Exactly twelve months later, in October of 2012, a late season tropical storm formed in the warm waters off Jamaica and began moving north. Fueled by warming oceans, the storm achieved hurricane status on October 24. Dubbed "Superstorm Sandy," she came ashore in New Jersey as a Category 2 hurricane, but what she lacked in windspeed she made up for in size and surge. While New York City and New Jersey suffered a direct hit, Connecticut's shoreline also flooded, and the state recorded wind gusts up to eighty-five miles per hour. Our trees, already weakened and hurting, fell with the rain. Thirty percent of the state's population lost power for days.

Our state's response to these dual disasters was not to improve the electrical grid or bear down on planning for and combatting climate change and its chaos. Rather, municipalities across the state began taking down trees: damaged trees, healthy trees, big trees, little trees. Any tree within twenty feet of a highway, byway, or powerline was selected and removed. Connecticut Routes 2 and 9 looked like clear-cut zones for timber interests. Tree-lined Elm Street in Rocky Hill, which had lost its namesake elms to Dutch elm disease years ago, now lost its giant shade maples and oaks. Even now, seven years after Sandy's destruction, the state highway crews still cut to stumps any trees daring to grow near Interstate 91. The landscape looks butchered. If we are going to awaken to this new consciousness, I hope we do it soon.

A nation that destroys its soils destroys itself. Forests are the lungs of our land, purifying the air and giving fresh strength to our people.

(HERMANN HESSE)

It seems it is human nature to blame victims for their own suffering, even when the victims are trees. Even when having more trees is part of the solution to lowering the level of carbon dioxide in the atmosphere. Even when lowering carbon output is vital to our own survival as a species. The ancient people of Easter Island cut down every tree that grew there, and then they, themselves, died out. We should pay attention and learn our lesson. We evolved long after the trees created a world hospitable to life on land. We will not long survive without their beauty and strength, their ability to store carbon and emit oxygen, the fruit they bear and the other creatures they provide life for. We must learn to listen, again, to the Earth.

One day, after a near miss on the highway that should have ended me—and somehow didn't—I brought my shaky self home to sit with my back against a strong-trunked tree. In delayed reaction, I wept adrenaline-laced tears at what had almost happened until I stopped trembling and grew calm. I felt the tree behind me, aging but still strong, and the solid earth below me. A sense of peace settled over me as I knew that one day (though not *that* day) I would be gone, but all that I saw in front of me—birds, bees, bushes—would go on living and procreating.

Aren't we blessed to have our days in the sun and rain, days when we grow and smile and cry and die, as all of life has ever done?

Reflection

I remember the first time I read Betty Smith's masterpiece *A Tree Grows In Brooklyn*, I was entranced by how her main character, Francie, mirrored the beautiful tree (an ailanthus) that flourished only in the poorest growing conditions.

If you judge humankind's relationship with trees through our references to them in our holy writings and art, and our pagan awe of groves and orchards, you must determine that our living is woven with theirs. Trees, like us, are energy vibrating as matter. We vibrate as skin and bones and feet and brains; they vibrate as bark and roots and branches and sap.

What is your spiritual connection with trees/forests? Are there trees that have figured prominently in your life? Journal or think about those stories. Realize what they mean or have meant to you. Ask the natural world (the trees or the sea, the prairie or the desert) to speak to you, to tell you its stories. If you listen, you may be called to provide healing how and where you can.

Earth Spirit
I am filled with gratitude
for the overarching shelter
of Your ever-spreading life.

15

Mother Bear's New Vista

Aging is not "lost youth"
but a new stage of opportunity and strength.

(BETTY FRIEDAN)

*G*ardening is my response to life. Whether I am experiencing joy or grief, anxiety or certainty, working in the garden steadies and calms me. It makes sense to my soul that I celebrate good news by adding new life to the land, assuage grief by noting life's persistence in the blossoming trees and perennials, and spill my fear and frustration into soil that can soak it up and transform it into something life-giving.

I went shopping for plants the other day. I have no extra money, and I should have used that time to write my thesis, but instead, I went to Garden's Dream and walked among the annuals, perennials, and herbs already out for purchase.

Four days before, I had learned that my thirty-three-year old daughter needed surgery to remove a 13-centimeter cyst from her uterus and left ovary. I learned there were other, smaller cysts, too. I learned that the large cyst was "complex" and would necessitate removal of her left ovary. I stopped sleeping soundly.

Two days later, I learned that the doctors were worried about cancer and so were preparing my daughter for the possibility of a complete hysterectomy. She and her husband came to visit for a few hours after that second doctor's appointment. Her gynecologist was getting oncology involved "just in case." I walked around holding my breath.

The morning I bought plants, I was really scared. My daughter was in a lot of pain. She had followed the doctor's instructions and called the practice to report the changes. The nurse left a message for her doctor, who was in surgery. Her doctor rushed my daughter's blood work and called her back.

While I waited, I sat down to write, but could not focus. I vacuumed the house. I scrubbed the kitchen. Finally, I went outside and began deconstructing a neglected flower bed. I pulled out a row of tiger lilies, six barely-emerging echinacea, and several still-unfurled ferns. I pruned the rose bush. I raked the ground and shoveled wood-chips over everything as mulch.

My back pocket buzzed. I read the text from my daughter: *Blood work shows no signs of malignancy. The cyst appears to be benign.*

I ran inside and up the stairs to my husband's office. I read him the text. We fell into one another's arm and wept our relief.

I did not realize how frightened I was until I wasn't any longer. Cancer had never been a major source of worry in our family until early this year, when it claimed my aged mother and young nephew within six weeks of one another. Suddenly, it was real. Suddenly, it was a threat to my own child.

While my mother was actively dying in January, and I was praying for a quick and painless end to her life, I was also begging God for the life of another of my children. I know nothing works that way. I believe that God loves us through this physical existence but is not in the habit of showing that love by saving one and not saving another. Nevertheless, I stood in the shower on one of those cold, sad mornings, bent over in grief and hiccupping with sobs, as I repeated over and over, "Please. I am begging you. I am begging you." That other child is also fine now. I thank God, though I know that nothing is a sign of Divine favor or disfavor.

Being a parent to adult children is an exercise in letting go of relevance. I can no longer demand that they eat their vegetables, or ground them for staying out too late. I cannot call them out of school for the day to ensure that they get some rest and recover from whatever is ailing them. I love them as fiercely and ferociously as I ever have. The mother bear still rumbles within me, all claws and fur and fangs. She sheaths those weapons now, though, and lumbers back into her cave until, unless, she is called upon. My children are not always appreciative of her force, and they don't want to be reminded of her presence. They want, and need, to direct their own lives, to make their own decisions and mistakes, and live and learn with what comes.

I want to say that this is fine with me, but that is not wholly true. It is fine with me when they buy a home, or take a new job, or decide to have a child, or not. It is not fine when I can see unhealthy risk in their decisions. That is when I bite my tongue before I utter words that dig a chasm between what I see and what they want to believe. That is when I choose the silence that makes relationship possible.

In a time of naked honesty, one of my children acknowledged an intentional distance kept between us. He had instituted the distance, and I had honored his choice, though I missed him. We didn't talk about it at the time, but as he watched my mother die, he brought it up.

"I have not been as close these last few years. I am sure you noticed it; you notice everything." A note of anguish crept into his voice, "I wanted to take care of my own problems. You're my mother for Chrissakes."

I watch my three children grow into adult relationships with one another that are built on respect and love. I am no longer at the center of their collective lives, no longer the center of my own family. My cubs have wandered off to find their own mates and bits of the world, leaving me to inhabit my space more fully. Mother Bear is out of her element, still full of strength, but without a channel for it. I have responded by immersing myself in myself, in my own dreams and aspirations. It is a strategy to find new life and a new *raison d'être*.

Garden work is life work for me. Planning, planting, and growing food and flowers fills me with purpose. I pour my determination and protective urges into the soil and around the plants I have welcomed into my yard. It reminds me that life, though ever changing, always endures.

We are not victims of aging, sickness and death. These are part of scenery, not the seer, who is immune to any form of change. This seer is the spirit, the expression of eternal being.

(DEEPAK CHOPRA)

So of course I went shopping for plants that day when I thought that life, as I know it, would continue. I set about seeing to it that I celebrated by buying catnip and collard greens; and then I wrote.

I am still writing as the story continues to tell itself. The threat of cancer is back, and my daughter will see an oncologist in three days. Again, I am not sleeping well, not breathing deeply. I offered to go with her, but her husband will take her, and I am glad for her for that. I will wait to hear from her, tending my garden, growling and crying my prayers, rising to stand and survey the untouched vista of the final third of my life.

Once, about a decade ago, I did some personal work with a local shaman who guided me through several journeys to other realms. In one vision I dropped through the ceiling of an ancient cave, landing on its hard dirt floor at the feet of a tall woman wrapped in a bear cloak. I asked her if she was my mother.

"No," she replied, "sister." She took my left hand and dropped a bear's tooth into my open palm.

In the vision I walked to the cave's opening high over a valley and saw a primeval forest spread out below me. I knew it was untouched by human beings, and I would be the first, and only, person to walk through it. I closed my hand around the tooth, and the vision took me to other places and times, just as time and life are doing now.

Reflection

It feels odd to be in my sixties when all pretense of youth and its strivings have passed. These last two years (the first two of my seventh decade) have been liminal for me. I don't really yet know how to be an elder; I've never been one before. When I look in the mirror I see an elder with some impressive wrinkles, and hair now as white as it is black. I have decided to look my age, though I really understand the desire not to.

These two years have been years of great loss and letting go, some forced and some voluntary. It is hard work, and like all hard work, it will change me. How it works out—well, we will have to wait and see.

Who do you want to be as an elder? Are you laying the foundation for that now? If you could describe yourself ten years from now, what would you look like? What would be important for you? Where would you find joy? How would your love manifest in the world? What do you need to let go of before that version of yourself can come into being?

Mother Spirit,
I know You understand the love
I bear for my children.
As they grow away from me,
may they grow deeper into You.
As I grow older,
may I too grow ever deeper ,
my roots sunk deep into Your soil.

Celtic Nature Prayers
Prayers from an Ancient Well

Find God in Nature
Pray for Our Endangered Planet

Long before they had heard about Christianity, the Celts knew that Nature was their portal to a great spiritual reality. Wells, mountain crags, caves, and lochs were "thin places" that allowed access to the realm of spirits. In these temples of Nature, the Celts sought physical and spiritual healing, as well as revelation. The salmon, the eagle, and even the tiny hazelnut, all were allies in helping humanity access the mysterious magic that underlay physical matter.

Paperback Price: $14.95

Kindle Price: $5.99

Water from
an Ancient Well

Celtic Spirituality for Modern Life

A Fresh Look at Celtic Spirituality

Using story, scripture, reflection, and prayer, this book offers readers a taste of the living water that refreshed the ancient Celts. The author invites readers to imitate the Celtic saints who were aware of God as a living presence in everybody and everything. This ancient perspective gives radical new alternatives to modern faith practices, ones that are both challenging

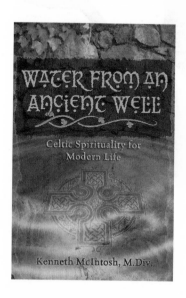

and constructively positive. This is a Christianity big enough to embrace the entire world.

Paperback Price: $19.99

Kindle Price: $7.49

Forest Church

A Field Guide to a Spiritual Connection with Nature

Brimming with insights and packed with information, this book draws you out, quite literally, into Nature to experience a new, well-thought-through pattern of spiritual practice. Bruce Stanley gives you all the resources you'll need, both practical and theoretical, to get going with a group or on your own.

Forest Church is a fresh expression of church drawing on much older traditions when sacred places and practices were out-side – but it is also drawing on contemporary research that highlights the benefits of spending time with Nature in wild places.

Paperback Price:
$14.75

Kindle Price:
$5.99

Anamchara
Books

ANAMCHARABOOKS.COM

Made in the USA
Middletown, DE
23 September 2020